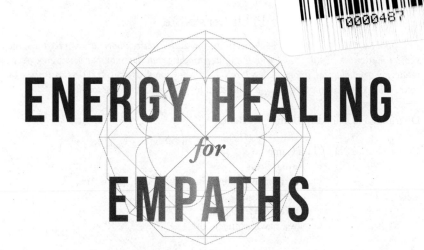

# ENERGY HEALING
### *for*
# EMPATHS

How to Protect Yourself from
Energy Vampires, Honor Your Boundaries
& Build Healthier Relationships

## LISA CAMPION

REVEAL PRESS
AN IMPRINT OF NEW HARBINGER PUBLICATIONS

# Publisher's Note

*This publication is designed to provide accurate and authoritative information in regard to the subject matter covered. It is sold with the understanding that the publisher is not engaged in rendering psychological, financial, legal, or other professional services. If expert assistance or counseling is needed, the services of a competent professional should be sought.*

Distributed in Canada by Raincoast Books

Copyright © 2021 by Lisa Campion
        Reveal Press
        An imprint of New Harbinger Publications, Inc.
        5674 Shattuck Avenue
        Oakland, CA 94609
        www.newharbinger.com

Cover design by Sara Christian; Acquired by Jess O'Brien; Edited by Kristi Hein

---

## Library of Congress Cataloging-in-Publication Data

Names: Campion, Lisa, author.
Title: Energy healing for empaths : how to protect yourself from energy vampires,
    honor your boundaries, and build healthier relationships / by Lisa Campion.
Description: Oakland : New Harbinger Publications, 2021. | Includes bibliographical
    references.
Identifiers: LCCN 2020031715 (print) | LCCN 2020031716 (ebook) | ISBN
    9781684035922 (trade paperback) | ISBN 9781684035939 (pdf) | ISBN
    9781684035946 (epub)
Subjects: LCSH: Self-defense--Psychic aspects. | Vital force.
Classification: LCC BF1045.S46 C36 2021  (print) | LCC BF1045.S46  (ebook) |
    DDC 615.8/528--dc23
LC record available at https://lccn.loc.gov/2020031715
LC ebook record available at https://lccn.loc.gov/2020031716

Printed in the United States of America

23    22    21

10  9  8  7  6  5  4  3  2

"I wish I could have read this book at age thirteen. It wasn't until I reached my forties that I had some notion of what it meant to be an empath. This book spells it out in relatable stories, exercises, and instruction that will help empaths of any age. Thank you for sharing your knowledge with us, Lisa. We've needed this book for a long time."

—**Jacob Nordby,** author of *Blessed Are the Weird* and *The Creative Cure*

*"Energy Healing for Empaths* is a highly entertaining and informative book that any sensitive person will benefit from reading. For highly sensitive persons (HSPs), empaths, and healers of any sort, it is a must-read. From a basic understanding of empathy to setting boundaries, from the rules of conscious relationship to highly effective energy clearing techniques for the healing professional, *Energy Healing for Empaths* covers all the bases!"

—**Cate Montana,** author of *The E-Word* and *Apollo and Me*

"Lisa delivers much-needed tools for empaths in a time we need them most. She describes the complications of energy cords within relationships in a way that makes it really easy to understand, and offers helpful practices to assist with boundaries and protection. Anyone who feels like they're too much of an emotional sponge for this world would benefit greatly from this book!"

—**Ora North,** author of *I Don't Want to Be an Empath Anymore*

"At last! An informative, easy-to-read, useful book that offers understanding and fresh insights to empaths and non-empaths alike. Read it and learn from Lisa, who has transformed her own energetic sensitivities into grounded superpowers."

—**Jac O'Keeffe,** author of *Born to be Free* and *How to Be a Spiritual Rebel,* and cofounder of the Association for Spiritual Integrity

"As an HSP myself, I wish I had read this book thirty years ago—it would have saved me decades of figuring it all out the hard way! Lisa Campion brilliantly breaks down the challenges and the gifts of the sensitive, empathic personality; and provides valuable insights, stories, and exercises to enable us to master our sensitivity. A must-read for anyone who has ever been told they were 'too sensitive'!"

—**Eileen Day McKusick,** author of *Tuning the Human Biofield* and *Electric Body, Electric Health*

"Lisa Campion has been a gifted healer, visionary, and teacher for more than three decades. She is committed to her own education—using the catch phrase, 'Guess what I learned, lately?' *Energy Healing for Empaths* offers much-needed insights, guidance, and inspiration for anyone who has long felt the strain or struggle of having an empathic nature. Her witty delivery had me laughing out loud; I highly recommend this book."

—**Sharon Wilsie,** founder of the Horse Speak Institute, author of *Horse Speak* and *Horses in Translation,* and Reiki master teacher

# Contents

# Foreword

"My hotel room is haunted! I have to get out of there."

Those were the first words Lisa Campion spoke to me, awakening in me a sisterly bond and an urgency to help her.

*She can't stay there*, I thought.

"There's an extra bed in my room…you're welcome to it," I said, looking into the wide brown eyes of my brand-new friend.

Lisa and I had been invited to be speakers at a summertime women's weekend retreat on a lake in Massachusetts, led by our mutual friend and colleague Wendy Capland. Amid the CEOs in swimsuits, shorts, and flip-flops; the tables of watermelon slices; and the coconut scent of Coppertone wafting in the air, I talked about the power of dreams and the hero's (aka Shero's) journey, and Lisa shared energy healing techniques with the women who run corporate America on the East Coast.

As she and I were packing up after the day's events, with still another day of the retreat ahead of us, I asked her, "Do you need company extracting your belongings from that haunted hotel?"—volunteering myself to be her wingwoman.

"That would be great!" She seemed to sigh with relief.

The next thing I knew, we were Thelma and Louise, speeding through the dark, bouncing in her SUV along the winding, tree-lined country roads, with nothing but starlight and adrenaline to guide us. Thankful for her high beams and the amber glow of the moon beaming hope through the windshield, we made a plan for how to get in and out as unscathed as possible from Hotel Hell.

I had to ask her what she had sensed was going on that had given her such a fright.

Lisa shivered, leaning forward, gripping the steering wheel. "I'm not sure exactly, but I got the sense my hotel used to be a brothel way back when…and let's just say, someone's or many people's lives came to an abrupt and not-so-happy ending in that room."

*Gulp.*

On the hour-long drive, trying not to get more spooked than we already were, I turned my curiosity to Lisa. I wanted to know about the life path that had led to her being such a powerful empath, psychic, and teacher. She shared with me that she had been sensitive from an early age, and she'd become a multiple black belt in karate to gain the mental and physical strength to cope.

"Being psychic as a kid didn't feel like a gift. If I could have, I would've given that gift back," she said, laughing.

But, thankfully, she wasn't able to give it back. In fact, thank God (for all of our sakes) she fell to her knees and said the prayer all empaths must declare at some point in their lives: "God, angels, guides, teaching spirits, ancestors, whoever you are and wherever you are, if I'm going to live in this crazy world with all its density, jagged edges, and energy vampires, then come out, come out wherever you are and help me do this!"

I nodded vigorously. I could relate, having had my own dark nights of the soul. In fact, I'm known for telling clients, "A crisis is a horrible thing to waste. If we become, as Margaret Mead suggested, the anthropologists of our lives, and remain conscious as we go through our breakdowns, we will discover they are predecessors to our great breakthroughs. In other words, if we look for it, we'll discover what we thought was the worst thing that could ever happen to us becomes the springboard for our purpose in life, the means by which we can make a true contribution to other people walking a similar path."

It's easy, in hindsight, to feel tidy, calm, and all put together on the days when the wind is at our back. But I believe that in the midst of a storm is when our ability to keep it together counts the most.

As we slowly drove down the block, I knew, without having to ask, which of the hotels on the block was spooking Lisa. She pulled up in front of a breathtakingly gorgeous Victorian inn with towers, turrets, and dormers, lit up by old-fashioned oil lamps. In spite of its outer aesthetic beauty, a wave of nausea filled my belly.

"Why is this street so abandoned?" I asked. "It's only 8 p.m. on a Friday night at the height of summer—in the center of town. Where are all the people?"

Lisa looked at me with a knowing face. *The spirits are keeping people away.* My new friend took some breaths and did a grounding exercise. I offered a prayer, calling on our angels, that we might be so bright that we could cast out any dark, stuck energy and elevate it to the light.

We tiptoed up the creaky wooden steps to the wrap-around porch. A note was taped on the door: "If you are a guest, use your key and let yourself in. There is no receptionist on the premises at this time. If you need assistance, call: xxx-xxx-xxxx."

We turned to each other. "That's so bizarre!" I'd never stayed at a hotel where there was no one working.

Even though everything in me wanted to run, I didn't want Lisa to have to face this alone—even though, now that I was more acquainted with her, I knew she was a spiritual baddass who could handle herself. Still, friends don't let friends go into public bathrooms—or haunted hotels—alone.

She fumbled in her purse and pulled out an old-fashioned key, fitted it into the lock, and turned the ornate doorknob. We crept into the lavish reception area, complete with Victorian-era decorative railings and carved newel posts.

"Hello!" "Hello!" Lisa and I called out to see if there were any humans there.

Getting no answer, we scampered up the plush carpeted staircase to the second floor. Walking down the hallway, we noticed all the doors to the other rooms were open…with no one inside.

*That's odd—why would all these doors be open?*

The place seemed completely empty...of people...who were...alive.

The door to Lisa's room was the only one shut and locked, as she'd left it that morning before coming to the retreat. She opened the door, which creaked on its hinges. All I could see was an old-fashioned dresser and a brass bed.

Lisa rushed into the sparse (albeit beautiful) room and in seconds assembled her belongings, throwing them into her luggage. We both said more prayers as we beat a retreat, like little kids running away from a Halloween haunted house.

Back in the car, we slammed the doors, and Lisa's shaking hand jiggled the key in the ignition. We couldn't screech out of there fast enough.

After leaving the former house of ill repute and the eerily quiet street in our dust, we both breathed a sigh of relief. The GPS spun out of control, extending the one-hour return trip to two hours, and our conversation meandered like the long road before us, filling each other in on the life paths that had led us to this bizarre juncture. I felt moved to ask her, "So, what's next for you? And how can I support you in wo-manifesting that?"

She blurted, "A book. Actually I have many books begging to be birthed. I love working one-on-one with clients and in small groups, but I really feel that I'm meant to contribute to more people. There are so many sensitive, gifted empaths in the world who are suffering—and I feel it's my mission to help them."

"Consider me your book midwife."

We made it back to the lake house, with the piney smell of the soft, rounded balsam fir needles welcoming us back from our adventure. We climbed the stairs to my room overlooking the sparkling water, shimmering in the warm breeze. Once Lisa was nestled into her twin bed on the lake side of the room, she said in a sleepy, raspy voice, "Ahhh...this room has a great vibe...sweet dreams."

Over the next year, I had the blessing of coaching Lisa on her journey from book conception to full-blown (wo)manifestation. Pulled by a vision and purpose, Lisa took guidance in the spirit of the medieval origin of her name, *champion*. Even more bravely than she had faced claiming her belongings from the haunted hotel, she faced her author demons—the ones that spring up for the best of us when we're completing the writing of a book, and especially once it's written, when it's time to hand it over to the public's scrutiny.

Eventually, last spring Lisa and I, along with the other midwives who had joined Team Lisa, celebrated *The Art of Psychic Reiki* being dubbed an instant Amazon.com #1 bestseller.

I'm sorry for whatever happened at that haunted hotel, and I pray that the souls who were trapped have found their way to the light. I like to think they did, as a result of Lisa's having been there that one night. Practicing what I preach—"A crisis is a terrible thing to waste"—I have to say I'm grateful for the bizarre experience that brought Lisa into my life, and for the honor of being asked to write this foreword to her second book, now in your possession (the kind for which you don't need an exorcism).

Whether you are familiar with or new to Lisa Campion's work, you are in for a treat. You'll find in reading *Energy Healing for Empaths* that you are in extremely capable hands. Lisa is a master teacher, gifted healer, and wonderful writer who will empower you to turn what you thought was a curse—your sensitivity—into your super-power.

If you are an empath who's struggled with anxiety, depression, and/or addiction; if you've had a difficult time setting boundaries; or if you seem to be a magnet for energy vampires, this book is for you—and the timing of your reading it right now could not be more perfect. As Lisa teaches (and I wholeheartedly concur), it is the empaths who will not only change but also inherit the earth.

Enjoy this book, and may it help you rise above the noise and haunted dwellings of this world, giving you the tools to alchemize all that's ever challenged you, so you may have the life you have thought was possible only in dreams. This is your time!

—Kelly Sullivan Walden
Author, *It's All in Your Dreams* and *The Hero's Journey Dream Oracle Cards*

# Prologue

When I was twenty, I met someone on a train who changed my life forever. It was 1985 and I was in my junior year of college. I had chosen to study abroad—in Aix-en-Provence in the south of France.

My friends and I had just spent a weekend in Paris and were on a late-night train on our way back to Aix. The train was packed, and we were all smooshed into a second-class carriage—practically sitting on each other's laps. I was stuffed into a corner, suffering the nightmare problems that any overstimulated psychic and empath would feel. (Though this being 1985, I had not yet heard the term *empath*.)

Being overly tired in cramped conditions with a bunch of exhausted and highly emotional people was overloading my sensitive circuits. I was a mess. The accumulation of everyone's emotions, energy, and physical proximity made me feel anxious and slightly nauseated.

Sitting directly across from me, our knees almost touching, was a handsome young man with intense, almost unblinking eyes. Looking back now over our conversation and subsequent friendship, I am sure that he was a *soulmate*, fulfilling his *soul contract* with me (two concepts that we'll explore later), and dropped in like a gift from above to set my life on a new track.

"Are you okay?" he asked me in French. "You look very uncomfortable. I can tell that you are a sensitive person and this is a hard situation for you. Too many people, too much energy all packed into a small place. But this is your nature and you must learn to deal with it. You *can* deal with it. You are meant to help a lot of people; I can tell that too."

He was very direct. There was no small talk and none of the flattering French charm that I had become accustomed to.

Remy was a few years older than I was, on his way to Marseille to visit his mother. For the past year he had been studying yoga and meditation in an ashram in India. I learned later that his mother was French and his father Israeli, and even though he was only twenty-five, he was one of the most conscious and spiritual people I have ever met. Remy was sent to me as part of the team of spiritual teachers that I have been blessed to have in my life. He showed up in the nick of time to help me learn what I needed to know to function as a young, untrained psychic and empath in a crowded and noisy world.

His teaching started that very night on the train, with three breathing exercises. (They became the foundation of the energy management techniques that I have taught to other empaths all over the world—and I will teach them to you in this book.)

"The first exercise," he told me, "is to clear energy when you have picked up too much." He explained that sensitive people are like a sponge, and the sponge needs to get wrung out. I was to do this once in the morning upon waking, at any time during the day when was I feeling overwrought, and once more before bed.

"The second exercise is to restore your energy when you are depleted. Sensitives have a permeable energy field and become easily depleted. You are tired all the time, yes? Especially when there is a lot of lights, noise, or drama around you?"

I readily agreed (and blessed my French professors and my immersion experience for helping me understand his rapid speech).

"The last exercise is to help you learn to protect yourself, since you are meant to be in the world. You can't retreat, *ma petite,* even if you want to. We must give you a kind of armor, a thicker skin against the difficulties of the world. You will live a life where you are walking into the difficulties of other people, so you need to be prepared."

And so, simply and wonderfully, I began to learn about both my empath nature and my healing path. At the very same moment, I was given three simple, valuable tools to keep me safe on that path.

\*\*\*

For the next ten years, Remy and I had something of a mystical hit-and-run connection. He would show up out of the blue; teach me the spiritual, energetic, and magical lessons he had learned; and then disappear again until the next time. Remy helped to give me direction in my life, the full set of tools I'll share with you, and the faith that help would be given when it was needed and that I was not alone on my journey. I want to instill that same faith in you. May this book be a lifeline for you, just as this chance encounter with a midnight magician was for me.

# Introduction

When a person tells me that they are an empath, I always want to say, "Congratulations—and I am sorry!" Being an empath is a double-edged sword. On one hand, it's an amazing gift—the gift of the healer. On the other, until we learn to manage our energy it's incredibly difficult to live as a sensitive person.

And in the beginning, before we understand our empath nature and learn some energetic skills, it can be especially bewildering and exhausting.

When I was in junior high school, I had a friend whose mom was really sick with cancer. I remember hugging this woman once and feeling everything she was feeling, all the sadness and pain and also the fierce love she had for her family. I could feel her physical pain too, and what it was like to be in her weakened state. I was thirteen years old, and I got the full-on hit of what it felt like to be a mother who was dying of cancer. She passed away soon after that, and then I could feel the pain of my friend and of everyone else in her house. It was overwhelming and incomprehensible, and yet in those moments I knew I wanted to do something to help. I knew that this experience was important, that life was made up of this kind of bittersweet reality, and that it all had something to do with my life purpose. I sensed that I was here in this life to help people like my friend and her family.

At this age, all my empathic tendencies were coming fully online, and I wasn't sure what to do with them. I couldn't understand why I wasn't like "normal" people. I tried to hide this aspect of myself, to fit in, because I was so afraid there was something really wrong with me. I worried that I might be going crazy.

When I was growing up in the 1970s and 1980s, there were no psychics on TV and no new age bookstores, and no one talking about what I was experiencing. I felt like a raw nerve, and everyone basically told me that I was too sensitive and that I should get a thicker skin. I cared too much, they told me. I was too emotional.

I was also experiencing a psychic opening that concerned me just as much as my empathic sensitivity. And just my luck: the psychic child of course slept in the most haunted room of a rather haunted old house, and I grappled nightly with spirit visitations that I never talked about. There are many different kinds of psychics, and I have always been a generalist as far as my abilities go. Some psychics are mediums who specialize in talking to people who have passed on. Other psychics read energy, see the future and the past, and commune with nonphysical beings like angels. I have always been able to do some of all of that, and I have struggled with trying to make sense of it all. I suspected that people who had experiences like mine sometimes ended up in a psychiatric hospital, so I kept quiet about all of it.

I was born with those psychic gifts: my very first memories involve seeing things other people didn't see. Because this was all so scary and uncomfortable, I spent the first twenty years of my life looking for the off switch. Eventually I did learn how to master both my empathic and psychic abilities. It was challenging, but I got help and teachers along the way, and I came to realize that all these skills were meant for one thing: to help me be a healer. Now, decades later, I am dedicated to helping other people learn to master their empathic, psychic, and intuitive gifts.

Because I had to learn to learn the hard way, any day that I can help someone else have an easier path than I did is a good day for me.

# Empaths Are Highly Sensitive People

One of empaths' special qualities is our high sensitivity to other peoples' energy, pain, and emotions. We actually *absorb* these—we are the psychic sponges of the world.

There are many very sensitive people all around us. Dr. Elaine Aron, author of *The Highly Sensitive Person*,[1] says that highly sensitive people (HSPs) make up 15 to 20 percent of the population. She points out that hard numbers are difficult to come by because high sensitivity is still not understood very well, or even believed in, by traditional Western medicine and psychiatry. Whatever the actual number, an increasing number of people are identifying as highly sensitive. It seems clear that HSPs have been part of our world all along, and we have only recently had terms that describe us as a group. I think too that more and more sensitives are being born now as part of our human evolution, so there are more aware sensitives than ever before.

In her groundbreaking work, Aron writes, "The highly sensitive person (HSP) has a sensitive nervous system, is aware of subtleties in his/her surroundings, and is more easily overwhelmed when in a highly stimulating environment." HSPs also tend to be rather shy and introverted. This set of behavioral and psychological traits, which Aron identifies as criteria for the highly sensitive person, primarily describes how the HSP processes sensory experiences and emotions.

Although the HSP is highly attuned to other people's emotions, the main defining characteristic of the HSP is the sensitivity of their sensory processing. HSPs notice subtle cues in the environment that others miss. (If you are curious about whether you meet the HSP criteria, Aron has a fantastic self-assessment test on her website, https://hsperson.com.)

Elaine Aron's work was a revelation for sensitives all over the world. Her careful description of HSPs has helped the highly sensitive people of the world understand themselves.

Our modern concept of empaths came out of Aron's work, and it highlights a difference in the way people experience being an HSP—or being an empath. The work of Dr. Judith Orloff, as detailed in her book *The Empath's Survival Guide: Life Strategies for Sensitive People*,[2] helps us understand the differences between the two types.

Empaths not only have the sensitive nervous system of an HSP but are primarily attuned to other people's emotional energies. Empaths feel *other people's feelings* as if they are their own. According to Dr. Orloff, they can also experience a physical and emotional backlash from this powerful attunement to others. The backlash might emerge as panic attacks, depression, or chronic fatigue that doctors can't find a cause for. In addition to the other-orientation that Orloff defines, I include in my definition of an empath greater intuitive and psychic capabilities. I feel that empath nature is a soul-level gift that is the foundation of an empath's life purpose.

Empaths also share the feeling that their emotional sensitivity is a curse, as it feels like a heavy burden. Yet we also have a soul-level knowing that our emotional attunement is a gift, one that makes us great healers, helpers, caregivers, and partners. It's a wild ride that can leave us feeling fine one minute and horribly depressed, anxious, or sad the next minute—just because we came in contact with someone else who is feeling those particular feelings.

So how can you tell if you are an empath? Many empaths share these qualities:

- You can feel what other people are feeling—either their emotions or their physical sensations, or both. This is more than noticing; you feel it as your own feelings.

- You are introverted. Big crowds of people make you uncomfortable. One-on-one interactions are better for you, and after you have been around people you need a lot of alone time to recover.

- You may prefer the company of small children, animals, or the natural world over that of other adults.

- You are very emotional. You often feel quite overwhelmed by your own emotions, and adding feeling other people's emotion onto that can swamp you with excessive emotion.

- You may experience more depression and anxiety than your peers, including social anxiety.

- You can easily be overwhelmed by sensory stimulation like lights, sounds, and fragrances. Any place that is crowded with people can blow your circuits!

- You are drawn to helping, healing, and caregiving. You have a very kind heart and tons of compassion; you really care. You may cry during heartwarming commercials, and you need to avoid violence in TV and movies.

- You are also highly intuitive and might be a little psychic, too. (We will be further defining those terms soon.)

- People frequently tell you that you are too sensitive or that you need to get a thicker skin.

If you see yourself in most of these descriptions, you can safely conclude you are an empath.

It's important to know that *this is normal*! There is nothing wrong, crazy, or bad about being an empath.

How you feel about this part of you often has a lot to do with whether you come from a family and culture that values sensitivity or rejects it.

There is great pain that comes with having such a core part of who we are rejected. Therefore much of what we are going to do in the book is to help you accept and love your sensitivity, so that you can see it for the gift that it is. Because being an empath is a gift to the world. But it can feel like a great big curse until we both accept and embrace our nature and learn to manage our energy.

## Empaths Are Healers

I often use the words *empath, intuitive, psychic, sensitive,* and *healer* to refer to the same kind of person. These words describe people gifted with a group of tools and gifts that are all meant for the same purpose: they are the tools that healers need. Empaths have all these qualities together in a package deal.

But just so we can all be on the same page, let's define some terms.

*Empaths* are people who absorb the energy of other people. It's an experience that goes much deeper than the empathy that most humans share. It's more than simply noticing that someone is having a feeling. If an empath is near someone who is experiencing a deep emotion, the empath will feel that emotion as if it is their own. This is called *emotional empathy.* (Again, this leads to a lot of confusion and suffering for empaths until we figure out that what we are feeling so strongly might not be *our* feeling, but someone else's.)

*Physical empathy* is experienced when an empath feels the physical sensations of another person in their own body. They might experience this when they touch someone or are in close physical proximity with them. They might also experience physical empathy when they are far away from someone they care about.

Here's an example. Abby is a massage therapist who always knows exactly where to put her hands on her clients. It seems like a miracle, since the client doesn't have to say anything. Abby just knows. She says, "As soon as I start the massage, I can feel in my own body what my client is feeling in theirs. I am not guessing; I feel their pain in my body, as if it were mine." And it's not just physical pain that Abby feels, but what is happening with her clients emotionally too.

"I can always tell when they are holding on to a stuck emotion, since I will suddenly get very sad when I am working on their shoulders or really angry when I am working on their hips," she said. "I feel it like it's my feeling, but I know it's theirs. It's a fantastic tool for me, since once I know, I can help them release it."

Abby beautifully describes how these two gifts—physical and emotional empathy—come together to help an empath be a healer. And until she realized how to clear herself after each session and also at the end of every day, she used to suffer from the physical and emotional pain that she brought home from work with her. Abby uses the energy management techniques that I will teach you in this book, and she is now thriving in her massage practice, pain free.

## Empaths Are Psychic and Intuitive

Let's expand on this a bit. Every empath I have met is also both very intuitive and psychic. (Not all psychics are empaths, but all empaths are psychic!)

So, what do I mean when I use these words?

*Intuition* is our inner knowing—information that comes from inside ourselves. Intuition has three components: the messages we receive from our own body, our feelings about things, and the certainty that comes from our gut. We don't know why we know; we just do. Or we might find ourselves saying something like, "I have a bad feeling about this" or "I knew that was going to happen!" Intuition is one of the best superpowers of an empath, since it helps us navigate the world, like a kind of sonar. It helps us steer toward things that are good for us and away from things that aren't. Intuition has been correlated to our animal instinct for survival, but it is also more than that.

*Psychic ability* helps us receive information from outside our systems. A more challenging concept for many to accept, the general idea is that we all (all humans, not just sensitives) have a team of spiritual beings who protect and guide us. Psychics learn to connect with these *spirit guides*. Although we always have actual living people who act as spiritual teachers, as Remy was to me, the term spirit guide refers to nonphysical beings whose purpose is to help us through both our daily and life and our spiritual journey. They can be anything from ancestors who connect to us from the other side, to angels, nature spirits, or even the spirits of animals. All of us have a team of these beings who are helping us from the sidelines, assisting us along the way.

People who have a strong psychic ability can get direct messages from these beings, maybe through dreams, or visions, as I do. Other people hear a voice in their head advising them about what direction to take in life. It could be as simple as hearing that voice remind you to take your umbrella today or really catching your attention when danger is present.

Many people get this information through feelings, hunches, knowings, and insights. As we develop our psychic ability, we become more and more conscious of these communications.

## Healing Is Our Calling

*Healer* is the broad term I use to describe someone who has a deep calling to help other people. Healers show up in all kinds of ways, many of them very ordinary. A healer might be a nurse or a kindergarten teacher; someone who tends a garden and creates herbal remedies; or someone drawn to traditional medicine, like a nurse or a physician. Ministers, therapists, chiropractors, and estheticians are often called to those helping professions from a deep desire to be of service to other people. And often it is empaths who feel this call.

Healers can also be called to work a very ordinary job, like in a big corporation. Healers show up in all walks of life and are people in all kinds of places. Here's an example.

On a recent trip, I missed my plane due to weather. I was a bit frantic, but I quickly realized that the man helping me at the ticket counter was an empath and a healer. He fixed my complex travel issue, found my luggage and rerouted it, helped me find a local hotel, and gave me an airline voucher for it. The whole time, he stayed calm and steady with me and with the dozens of other people he was helping. At one point, he touched my shoulder, and I felt a surge of calming, healing energy flowing from him.

I asked him if he liked his job.

"I love it," he said. "I love helping people more than anything, and people who are traveling often need help. It can be scary, and it seems like no one cares. I care, and I can help."

He was like an angel at the ticket counter, and I heard a whole line of people tell him so. He glowed with calm and happiness as he sorted out people's worst travel nightmares. He was a fantastic healer!

## About This Book

Now that we are all on the same page as to what an empath is—and who this book is for—let's turn to what this book is about.

Being an empath truly is living with a gift that's both a blessing and a curse. In chapter 1, we will be looking at the double-edged sword that being an empath can feel like. We will examine all the challenges that we face, such as having a sensitive nervous system that can easily throw us into overwhelm. It helps to understand how the maturity or immaturity of our soul affects our level of sensitivity, so we will explore the idea of how being a new soul, a middle soul, and an old soul helps create our empathic natures.

An empath's emotional life can be a wild ride. We have our own intense emotional natures, which can lead to issues like anxiety, depression, and addictions. In chapter 2, we will be learning how to manage our emotions in an empowering way so that we are not repressing them or flooding uncontrollably. In the center of that seesaw is how we can contain our strong emotions in a healthy way, one in which we don't take our intense emotions out on other people. It's on us to learn to handle our emotions in an empowered way, and we will go through how to do that, step by step.

Once we have a grip on our emotions, it's critical that we learn powerful energy management fundamentals so that we can ground ourselves in the face of other people's energy and emotions. Chapter 3 lays out these fundamentals, which include how to clear the energy that we absorb from others and how to replace our lost energy when we leak it out. And we will uncover some easy and effective methods for protecting ourselves by creating a strong energetic barrier between us and the world.

Now that we have a strong foundation to stand on in our energy and emotions, we face the next challenge; how do we hold onto ourselves in our most difficult relationships? Chapter 4 shows us how to dance with the people who are the most draining to us: the energy vampires. We all have those difficult people in our lives, and we need effective strategies for recognizing and handling the three different types of energy vampire. We will cover how to spot the most dangerous type—the predatory energy vampire—and what to do if you encounter one. We also need skills to manage the more prevalent victim type energy vampire. There are also the situational vamps, who fall into energy-sucking tendencies when they fall on hard times, often due to no fault of their own. Forewarned is forearmed, and once we know how to spot these different types, we will discuss how to extricate yourself from these challenging relationships and how to handle them powerfully even when you can't.

It's all about setting boundaries, but what's an empath to do when we don't even know what a boundary really is? Chapter 5 brings us concrete measures to defend our space against invaders of all kinds. The ability to say the word no is something most sensitives have to acquire, and we will discuss how to use anger and resentment as two potent signals that you need to set a boundary. We will also examine ways to do extreme boundary setting for the most challenging of situations, because sometimes we just need to walk away.

Empaths have a conundrum when it comes to love, sex, and relationships. We can be at our most powerful in relationships, or we can be at our most vulnerable and sustain real damage. Empaths in love need special skills and tools so we can manage our energy and not get lost in our intimate relationships. And sex creates unique opportunities to either find joy and bliss or get the life drained out of you. In chapter 7, we will discover how to embrace our love relationships without getting totally lost in them and how to manage our energetic boundaries in our sexual relationships.

Finally, what happens when an empath gets so drained that we become an energy vampire ourself? It happens all the time, but we can recover. We can avoid becoming an energy vampire when we know how to live a life that deeply sustains us. Creativity, play, and time in nature and meaningful communities, as well as a spiritual practice can help make living as an empath the joy it was meant to be.

When we fully embrace our gifts and celebrate our empathic natures, we can create a life that is rich and full of pleasure and meaningful service to others, too. Thank you for joining me on this journey, I look forward to being your guide and celebrating with you as you come more and more into loving and accepting your empath nature.

Let's dig in!

# CHAPTER 1

# The Gift That Feels Like a Curse

Lily is an empath who first came in to my office for a Reiki session and a psychic reading. She was suffering with chronic pain and a host of physical issues she couldn't explain. She is twenty-eight and works in human resources at a big corporation. She was drawn to human resources because she is one of those people who truly loves helping others. She is also a single mom to her son, Adam. Lily is a gentle soul, with large brown eyes and a huge heart. She loves connecting with the pets, little kids, and elders in the apartment complex where she lives. With what little spare time she has, she volunteers at an animal shelter.

When we met, her big heart and all her responsibilities had left her chronically tired and energy-depleted. She also suffered from anxiety, especially around large groups of people or in crowded places like bars and restaurants. So she concluded that she had social anxiety. Yet Lily is very skilled at relating to people, and, like most empaths, she has genius-level emotional intelligence. She much prefers one-on-one connections with people in quiet environments, and she loves to share deep feelings and thoughts. She is a great listener, and anyone lucky enough to get some one-on-one time with her feels comforted, seen, and heard by her.

On her good days, Lily is in love with life, humanity, and the whole world. It is as if she is made of love, and everyone who encounters her has a healing experience. Her empathic nature gives her a deep knowing that we are all one, everything is connected, and the universe is made of love.

On her bad days, Lily is swamped with the backwash of other people's stuff. It feels like she is drowning in bad energy and strong emotions. She is a magnet for anyone who is in physical pain and needs healing, and she tends to take on their pain. Her friends call her when they need to talk to someone; strangers approach her in the supermarket and tell her their whole life story. In challenging environments— like the crowded subway, supermarkets, and Adam's daycare—she struggles with fatigue and anxiety. The complexity of life overwhelms her.

Lily also suffers from a variety of pain issues that her doctor has lumped together in a diagnosis of fibromyalgia. She has food allergies and chemical sensitives that lead to frequent and debilitating migraines. When we met, she was also beginning to notice that she is very sensitive to electromagnetic radiation (from WiFi routers, computers, cell phones, and fluorescent lights).

Lily seems to attract difficult relationships into her life. Her energy vampire boss puts her down, takes credit for her work, and disgorges her personal issues all over Lily. Energy vampires are those people who seem to suck the very life out of us, and many empaths are energy vampire magnets, as Lily was. (You'll find a full exploration of energy vampires and what to do about them in chapter 4.) Lily's mother is needy, energy-hungry, and rather childlike herself. Lily has had to be the "parent" in the relationship starting from when she was about eight years old. Lily has also had a string of relationships with needy men who are drawn to her compassionate, healer nature. They come needing help and without much to contribute, treating her as if she is a therapist rather than a life partner. Lily has a hard time setting boundaries with these people because she is kindhearted, she can feel their pain, and she hates conflict more than anything.

"I am a mess!" Lily told me. "I am sick, tired, and anxious all the time, and I have no idea why. I really think there is something seriously wrong with me, and I am worried that I might actually be crazy."

# If This Is a Gift, Can I Send It Back?!

Lily's story is very typical of what most empaths go through until they learn to manage their energy. It's all so challenging, and so overwhelming, that we often wish there was a return policy on this gift! There isn't, of course. But if we fully understand the challenges, we can find a way to work through them, protect ourself, and use our gifts. It's possible for you to go on the same journey of empowerment that Lily took, and I promise to share with you the amazing transformation that Lily went through in the conclusion of this book.

We can break down our challenging issues into a few overlapping categories: those we face with others, those we face with our environment, and those we face with our own internal responses to those things. All three contribute to the sensory and emotional stress that I call *empathic overload*.


# Empathic Overload

If empaths are the psychic sponges of the world, *empathic overload* is the signal that the sponge is totally saturated. This can happen any time we are surrounded by chaotic and busy energy: when we are traveling or are at the movies, in shopping centers, in hospitals. Even places that are meant to be fun for people, like amusement parks, can overload our circuits. Spending time with a group of people can have the same effect.

Empathic overload happens to me about twenty minutes into any big-box store or shopping mall. The crowds, fluorescent lights, chemicals, perfumes, and visual overstimulation blow a circuit in my energy system, and I become numb, cranky, dissociated, and forgetful.

Let's take a look at the symptoms of empathic overload so you can recognize it when you are in it:

- Physical exhaustion. You feel so tired that you could lie down and take a nap in the middle of the store.

- Mental confusion and brain fog. When you enter a store, you forget everything you meant to buy.

- Feeling emotionally drained or swamped. You simply cannot process one more feeling.

- Feeling numb, dissociated, and spacy. Your attention span is shot.

- Headaches, even migraines.

- Anxiety and irritability. You feel like a raw, exposed nerve.

Returning from a day out, an empath may need a good cry, or a nap, or both. Empathic children can be limp and cranky when they get home from school. We all will seek quiet alone time to try and shake off the emotions and stress we soaked up when we are out and about. In chapter 3 we will fully cover how to wring out the sponge using our energy management fundamental exercises. Now let's examine how we handle being around others.

## The Challenge of Over-Giving

People! We love them, yet we can feel we're at their mercy. They are both the source of our life purpose and also the reason that we want to hide under beds, live by ourselves in a hut in the woods, or jump off the planet, depending on how our day is going.

Because all empaths have the soul of a healer, people who need healing are attracted to us, like moths to a flame. We are all very skilled at reading other people's energy, mostly unconsciously. So I have observed that needy people can unconsciously feel an empath's kind heart and permeable boundaries. Many empaths have told me that other people will walk up to them in public places and lay out their whole life story. When you have excellent boundaries, this is fine, but our naturally porous natures mean that we have to work extra hard to establish boundaries. We will work through this in several chapters of this book, but I wanted to start out by acknowledging that people, as much as we love them, are a big source of our problems, at least until we learn to better protect ourselves.

The bigger your heart is and the worse your boundaries are, the more people will pull on you as a way to fill their energy needs. Almost all empaths have the painful habit of over-giving in our relationships. It continues to surprise me that many empaths have never considered that they can set a boundary by saying no to people. When I suggest that they can, I often get an incredulous *You can do that?* look.

This habit of over-giving can be chalked up to the enormous compassion that empaths naturally feel. Empaths have big hearts, and we deeply, genuinely care about other people. Those big, compassionate hearts are ever ready to see the good side of people and to give everyone a second, third, or even a hundredth chance.

Since we genuinely feel someone's need and pain in the moment, it's so hard to say no, and we over-give. We join that extra committee, we take the box of abandoned puppies, we "adopt" the hurting people of the world, forgetting that as we say yes to all of that, we are overcommitting our limited energy, time, and resources. And therefore we become drained, empty, tired, and sick.

## Trapped by Being Too Nice

Here is the big dilemma that empaths face when dealing with other people. Conflicts are very hard for us, so we err on the side of being too nice. When we finally have had enough, we take a big risk, say no, and set a boundary. Saying no to others feels so mean, especially when our tender hearts easily feel their pain and their need. Empaths often feel as if our very worth depends on our service to other people. When we set a healthy boundary and choose not to be of service in that moment, we can feel shame and guilt.

And then we are stuck with not only our own guilt and shame, but also the hurt, anger, and disappointment of the person whose request we turned down. It's a horrible confluence of intense feelings that are hard for an empath to process. In the short run, it feels easier to suck it up and say yes then to deal with the perfect storm of emotional backwash after we say no.

However, in the long run saying yes to every request is not a great plan, because it leads to burnout and a loss of a sense of ourselves and being the top priority in our own life. We must learn to handle both our own emotions and the emotions of the person we have said no to.

My friend Judy described how she needed to set a boundary with her housemate. Things were getting out of hand in the house, and her housemate wasn't pulling his weight. Judy felt bad for him because he was going through a difficult breakup, so she let things pile up before she confronted him.

> When I finally did put my foot down, he was surprised and upset. I had been letting things slide for a while, so it must have come out of the blue and seemed unreasonable to him. Although he was the one who was not tuning in to how his behavior was affecting the other people in the house, I felt like I was the jerk for saying something about it, even though he was the one who was behaving badly. I actually felt like I was being so mean by pointing out the fact that his behavior was unacceptable, like I should have been polite and continue to let it slide.

Judy learned an important lesson on holding a boundary, speaking our truths, and not falling into the empath trap of being too nice. That's an essential skill set for us to feel fully empowered in the world.

## Environmental Overwhelm

Empaths can also be strongly impacted by our physical environments. Consider some of the more difficult environmental challenges we face. Lights, noise, and other sensory stimulation has a profound effect on our nervous systems, as does the residue of people's emotions, experiences, and actions that can energetically imprint on a place. The material of physical locations—like bricks, wood, cement, and fabric—will absorb all kinds of human energy and hold that residue. Those places seldom get cleaned up on an energetic level.

The other day I got into a cab in Boston. It was filled with a miasma of residual energy, like horrible cologne left over from the last few hundred people who had been in the cab. I thought of all the things that happen in cabs: people fight, make out, or head urgently to the airport, stressing about being late, just as I was doing. In addition to the mental and emotional imprint, people leave body fluids—sweat, blood, tears, drool—on the permeable fabric of the cab interior that holds a massive amount of energetic residue. It was almost unbearable, and I felt like asking the cabbie to pull over so I could break out my smudge stick and clear the cab.

In lieu of this, I whipped out a small vial of fragrance-free flower essences that I carry in my bag for just this type of psychic emergency. A few drops of Clear Light 2 (from Petaltone USA), and the cab was clear as it was ever going to be. Flower essences are made by putting flowers in distilled water for a period of time in a process that extracts the vibrational essence of the plant. They are not essential oils, which have a fragrance. They have a powerful but subtle effect on people and environments, and I often use them when I am clearing energy from people and environments. I considered it my community service action of the day. I did the same thing in the airport waiting lounge, the plane itself, and the hotel room I stayed in at my destination. I have also done this in the courthouse while I was on jury duty, hospital emergency rooms, and scary restrooms across the world.

The spaces we occupy generally fall into three categories. There are places that generally have wonderful, clear, uplifting energy, like churches, gardens, and meditation centers. Some places have intensely chaotic energy that is both good and bad, all mixed up together. I find that places like airports, shopping malls, and movie theaters fall into this category. And there are places with blazingly negative energy, where the misery of generations has stained the environment permanently. Prisons, mental hospitals, battlefields, and crime scenes hold powerful negative imprints that deeply affect empaths. (A few years ago, I had my psychic circuits blown on a tour of a castle in the Scottish Highlands. The dungeon was bad, holding the energetic residue of death, pain, and suffering, and the tour guide bragged about how many people had died there. But I was not expecting to get bowled over in the bedrooms until our tour guide told us about a series of murders that had taken place there.)

On the other hand, we can completely restore our delicate energy systems when we visit places that have loving, high vibration and peaceful energy. Most empaths know that a walk on the beach or in the woods is restorative, and I also find any place devoted to beauty will refill my energy tanks.

Another strong environmental challenge to empaths is the level of toxicity that exists in the world these days. Because of our spongy boundaries and general sensitivity, empaths are highly impacted by chemicals like food additives, cleaners, and artificial fragrances. Radiation from microwaves and WiFi is another problem for many sensitives, as well as the electromagnetic frequencies (EMFs) emitted by fluorescent lights, cell phones, and computers. The strong, toxic chemical and EMF soup that we live in can sap an empath of strength, and non-empathic people may not be aware of this. (Fortunately, WiFi radiation can be reduced by turning off routers at night and during any extended periods of disuse.)

Eating as cleanly as you can is good advice for all of us—and particularly important for empaths. Eat organic food as much as possible. Empathic children, with their growing bodies and brains, seem to be very sensitive to food additives; they may have food allergies and other sensitivities. These kids may be more vulnerable to food additives like food coloring and preservatives, GMO foods, and foods carrying a heavy pesticide chemical, like conventionally grown wheat, corn, and soy.

It's important to learn what environmental pollutants you are most sensitive to and reduce them in your environments. Avoid household cleaners with harsh chemicals; there are gentler natural alternatives. And the good news is that as we strengthen ourselves with our energy training, we gain greater immunity to these toxins.

Let's take a look at the physical effects that our sensitivity can lead to.

## Physical Illnesses

Empaths' extra-sensitive natures can take a toll on our bodies. In general, we have delicate constitutions that are easily thrown off kilter. Many empaths learn a habit of *somatizing* when they are children, which means that they learn to run their emotions through their bodies rather than feeling them as emotions.

This happens if you grow up in a family where it is not okay to have your emotions as a child. Maybe when you became emotional you were told that you were too sensitive; you got scolded, yelled at, or worse. If your deep feelings as a child pushed your parents over the edge of what they could handle, you might have learned to stuff your feelings and make your body process them.

This habit of somatizing our feelings creates lifelong physical issues in the body until we learn to process our emotions in a more direct and productive way. We process empathic overload in the same way, until we learn better ways.

Our bodies filter toxins through five organ systems:

- Kidneys and bladder

- Lungs

- Skin (skin and lung conditions often go together, as with asthma and eczema)

- Liver and gallbladder

- The digestive system, including the stomach and small and large intestines

These systems also work very well to filter emotional toxins. Unfortunately, using them to filter our emotions creates chronic health problems. Think about your own health issues and your physical constitution and see if any of these filtering organs are weak spots for you. An empath may have a "nervous" stomach from running their emotions through their gut, or, like me, have a constant battle with their gall bladder and liver.

As well as processing all our emotional residue through these body systems, empaths can also have other health issues:

- A weak immune system, stemming from our spongy boundaries

- Autoimmune issues, which come from sensitivity to toxins and sometimes from self-rejection and shame

- Conditions like fibromyalgia, which can arise when unprocessed emotional pain, usually from unhealed emotional trauma, is held in the nervous system

- Migraines, which can arise from using our mind to push down our emotions

- Sleep disturbances that are stress and anxiety related

Of course, we need to handle our physical issues using common sense. Seek good medical help for all health issues, and get the best that Western medicine can offer. But it's wise to look at how our emotions and energy contribute to our physical health. Generally speaking, if you have physical symptoms for which the doctors can't find a medical reason, you can assume that your symptoms are emotional and energetic.

Many empaths experience huge health improvements as they establish stronger boundaries and better energy management practices and when they learn to process their emotions in healthier and more direct ways.

Our next challenge moves us into the realm of our mental health.


## Emotional Strain

One of the biggest pain points for empaths is that our emotions run wild and can be extreme. Learning to regulate our emotional states is fundamental to being healthy in the world, but sadly, most empaths have no idea how to do this. We feel our own emotions deeply and we can go to extremes, experiencing very high highs and scary low lows. Add the fact that we feel everyone else's emotions and sensations, and empaths can become an emotional hot mess.

When empaths get overwhelmed by emotions, our own and others, we can experience a host of emotional problems including anxiety, depression, and addiction. Empaths also need to clear up any possible past trauma. The worse that trauma is, the more intense the emotional overwhelm it triggers. Empaths must learn to deal with our emotions every day in a healthy and productive way and commit to cleaning up any past traumas that we have suffered. You'll learn how to do this in the next chapter.

I am sure that as a sensitive you have experienced some of these challenges. I acknowledge and honor what you have been through. Fortunately, there are also powerful gifts that come with being an empath, so let's take a moment to look at the bright side. Healing our past trauma and learning to manage our energy will lead us to our power—and it is very good power.

## Being an Empath Is a Gift, to Ourselves and to Others

To be fully empowered in a world where there are many natural energy-takers, we must learn and embody one important truth: we are each responsible for managing our own energy, and no one else can do it for us. There is tremendous empowerment on the other side of feeling victimized, and it's worth doing all the inner work that we need to in order to get there.

### Letting Go of the Victim Identity

Empaths tend to feel victimized by the world and all the people in it. For example, does it seem to you as if the holidays were specifically designed to torture and drain you? The overstimulation of shopping, the requests for giving more and more—these can throw an empath into a state of exhaustion and overwhelm. It's all too easy to feel like the world is out to get you; to ask *Why me?!*

I have seen some empaths wear this victim status as a badge of honor and really work the "poor me" angle. I am not dismissing the impact that being highly sensitive in our tough world can have on a sensitive person, but living in the victim place doesn't feel very good, nor is it a useful and empowering stance.

I recently taught a group of empaths at a workshop on managing your energy. A middle-aged woman named Susan dramatically announced to the group that she was the most sensitive empath ever and that she needed special accommodations. Susan needed extra pillows and a special seat, the temperature in the room to be just so, and she needed everyone to keep a certain distance away from her and not touch her at all so she wouldn't be flooded with their energy. Clearly, she was deeply enjoying all the privileges and attention that came with being so special.

A few of the other women jumped up to give her exactly what she needed, sympathizing all the way with her pain. I am not saying that she wasn't really an empath, but I knew that the quiet ones responding to her were the most empathic people there.

To claim our power as empaths, we must give up feeling victimized and learn to step into our powers. The key to this is learning to manage our energy, set powerful and effective boundaries, and fully own that we are healers. Here are some very empowering truths for you:

- It's your responsibility to learn to manage your energy. No one else can do this for you, and expecting other people to take over this area of your life is disempowering and unrealistic.

- It's up to you to set your boundaries and say no. Most people are thrilled to let you over-give to them and won't stop you from doing so.

- We train people how to treat us. If they are used to our over-giving, that is what they expect.

- We can also retrain them to expect less from us, but it takes a while for this to sink in.

# EMPATHY IS A GIFT TO THE WORLD

Although we need all types of people here on our planet, I am convinced that the world would be a kinder and gentler place if we had more empaths.

- Empaths are naturally compassionate. We automatically put ourselves in others' shoes and think about how they are going to feel before we speak.

- Empaths are nonviolent and cannot abide another's suffering. We have a deep inner knowing that we are all connected, so hurting another means hurting oneself.

- We are natural stewards of the planet and are drawn toward caretaking animals, gardens, and nature.

- We know that the planet is an alive, conscious being and that our well-being is connected to that of every other living thing in an interdependent web of life, even when it's not obvious.

- For empaths, there is no hierarchy of whose life is more important. If you protectively move spiders out of harm's way and return rain-stranded worms to the soil, you share this feeling.

- We are also drawn to the people most in need of nurturing and protection, like babies, small children, the elderly and infirm, and people at the end of life.

I am convinced that the world would be a better place for all if empaths were in charge!

- When you start setting boundaries, your people might be unhappy about it. But if you are consistent and kind about it, over time they will get used to it.

- When we have a firm and consistent boundary, others begin to respect us. No one really respects a doormat. Empaths are often shocked to find that they get more respect when they get good at setting boundaries.

It's liberating to know that we can take control of our energy, set boundaries, say no, and decide when, where, and what we are willing to give from our hearts. It takes a lot of work for most empaths to do this, and the impulse to blame it all on the "energy vampires" is strong, but this will not move you forward in your life. We must all be fully responsible for our boundaries and our flow of energy.

## Empaths Are Old Souls

The empath's spiritual gifts of compassion, nonviolence, and commitment to serve humanity and the world are strong indicators of an old soul. I believe that our souls mellow into being more and more compassionate as we spend time incarnating here on planet Earth. The longer our souls are embodied in the world, the more empathic and sensitive we become. As a psychic, I am always seeing people's past lives, so I believe in reincarnation. If you don't, that's okay; you can perhaps see the past lives concept as a metaphor or an experience of our archetypal self.

I want to take a moment to honor the old soul in you, for you are a gift to the world. It seems that more empaths are being born now than ever before, and that so many of us are waking up to our gifts. Empaths are highly compassionate and usually nonviolent. Since we really feel and know in our hearts that we are all one, all connected to each other and the planet itself, we choose love, interconnection, and nonviolence. For the most part, we choose humanitarian ideals and strive to live in harmony with animals, plants, and the earth itself. We value life and love above all else.

I hope you will find a way to accept your nature as an empath and fully live in the power of it. Much of that comes from knowing and living our life purpose as healers. And it also means making lifestyle choices that fully support us. When we do this and don't try and pretend to be someone else, we can live in the world comfortably and with power.

## Fully Thriving as an Empath

When you can accept your nature as an empath, you can seek to live a life in harmony with your core nature. Each empath has unique needs, but here are some common themes for what we all need in order to thrive:

- Commit yourself to a daily energy management practice. This will help you ground yourself, clear off the energy that doesn't belong to you, and refill your spent energy. There are many practices to choose from in chapter 3.

- Find ways to spend time alone. Solitude is a balm to the soul of an empath; claim this need and be unapologetic about it.

- Commune with nature. Most empaths have a strong affinity for nature, and it's very healing and reviving to connect with the natural world.

- Eat clean and lower your chemical load. Empath are more sensitive than others to chemicals and radiation. Ditch the microwave, and turn off your WiFi at night. Spend some extended time away from EMF radiation if you can.

- Establish a daily practice of handling your emotions. As they come up, you can manage them in a healthy, productive way. Write in your journal, scream in your car, or get therapy if need be. Cry when you need to. Don't feel bad about it; it's a primary need for empaths.

- Find community. Even though most empaths are fairly introverted, it helps us to be among like-minded people. Join a healer's group, learn Reiki, or find a meditation group. Start a meetup for empaths in your area.

- Live your life purpose. Discover your unique set of gifts and find a way to use them in the world. Most of you will not become a professional healer with an office doing clinical work the way that I do, but you can find your own way of contributing.

- Keep your spirit happy by having a spiritual practice that works for you. Go to church, do a prayer circle, practice yoga, do a daily meditation, spend time immersed in nature or a garden.

When we live from these basic principles in our lives, being sensitive stops feeling like a terrible burden and becomes a source of soul-level pleasure and satisfaction. Figure out what you really need, then give it to yourself.

## The Maturity of Our Soul's Journey

As a psychic, my talent is to see people at the level of the soul—your soul being that core essence that doesn't change between lifetimes. Each soul embarks on a journey, a narrative that is fascinating to me. Looking at our experiences and relationships from this soul's-eye view can give us clarity on issues that seem hopelessly tangled otherwise. In doing thousands of psychic readings over the years, I see a pattern in our souls' development. From it I have developed a very empowering theory all my own. Feel free to take whatever resonates and leave the rest.

Here is my theory: planet Earth is a training planet for warrior souls—a sort of boot camp—and if you are a warrior soul, this is a really fun place to be. Warrior souls are by nature fighters, heroes, defenders, and protectors. They have many beautiful qualities, like courage, leadership, and the ability to take bold, decisive action. On their bad days, they can be argumentative, seeing everything as a battle in a me-versus-you way.

This planet has some singular properties that make it a powerful place to learn, especially for the warrior soul types. The laws of this dimension that shape our experience here are polarity, free will, physicality, cause and effect, and finally the law of karma. Let's look at each in turn.

- The law of polarity posits that the earth is a polarized place—that everything here has an opposite. Thus we experience the dual natures of the shadow and the light, good and evil, light and dark, and so on.

- The law of free will states that we are allowed to choose among all the possibilities this polarized world offers us.

- The law of physicality means we take physical forms—our human bodies with all our powerful emotions and sensations.

- Through the law of cause and effect, with these physical bodies we experience the results of our choices.

- The law of karma means we get to carry the imprints, relationships, and lessons of our experiences from one lifetime to another.

It's a clever setup and, as far as I can tell, the only one like it in the universe. According to these laws, we are meant to choose and then to learn by experiencing the results of our choices in a very emotional and physical way.

In soul form we are good at conceptual learning, but we need the body, with all its emotions and sensations, to actually *experience*. This is like the difference between reading a recipe, which is a concept, and cooking and eating the dish, which is an experience. We need a body and all its sensory apparatus to experience the food in all its glory. And we need our emotions, produced by the endocrine system, to experience pleasure and joy and to give the meal meaning and context.

Add to the mix the law of causality, and we also get to experiences the consequences of our choices and actions. If you jump off a cliff, you will experience the results of gravity and probably die. Lesson learned!

The law of karma means a carrying over from one lifetime to another. I see karma as leftovers: whatever you didn't finish learning in this life, you carry with you until you do finish it. We collect positive karma when we master things and are compassionate in our choices; we rack up negative karma when we don't.

New souls come into this dimension in a pretty raw state. They crave experience and generally learn things the hard way. New souls have some really good qualities: they are highly creative and often bring new ideas and experiences to this planet. They are definitely fun to party with. New souls are hungry for the experience of power, sex, and money; if you're familiar with the *Game of Thrones* series, that gives you a good sense of what new souls are all about. I think people like Tesla inventor Elon Musk are new souls. They try new things, and they can be genius at breaking rules and paradigms. New souls are usually charming, seductive, and a whole lot of fun. They are pleasure seekers, without empathy or remorse, or any idea that their actions have consequences for other people. They crash around, jockeying for position and goodies; they haven't learned that there is a real price to be paid.

One type of new soul is the predatory energy vampire, which we will discuss in chapter 4. Seeing them as new souls can help us understand their behavior. They can't choose another way to behave, since they are basically rank beginners here on planet Earth. New souls rack up karma, which they then must start to balance out during their middle soul experience.

The middle soul stage of development is in some ways the most difficult and certainly the most painful to go through. At least a new soul has a lot of fun, even if it's a walk on the wild side for many of us who live with them. In our middle soul lifetime we have to start paying the bill for all the fun we had in our new soul days. We choose to experience "now the shoe is on the other foot" lifetimes. This means that if, as a new soul, you bought slaves and didn't treat them very well, you might choose to have an experience as a slave in your middle soul lifetime.

Choices like this one teach us compassion in a very experiential way. New souls here truly learn only through having a direct experience. A "shoe is on the other foot" experience teaches us directly that "this actually sucks—it doesn't feel nice at all to be treated as if I am less than human." The evolving soul learns compassion from firsthand experience.

According to the law of polarity, we need to experience both sides of any polarity to fully understand it. We have lifetimes in which we have total power and control over another person in our new soul flesh and other lifetimes in which we are totally dominated by another. We play both the victim and the victimizer in our pursuit of compassion and understanding.

These victim lifetimes are extremely difficult to live through, but ultimately they lead to some important lessons. We learn deep compassion for others' suffering, and we have an opportunity to learn that we always have the power to choose how we respond to the things that happen to us. Yet in the midst of middle soul lifetimes, we may feel victimized and confounded by misery and suffering that we can't seem to find a way out of. Because middle soul people haven't yet learned to empower themselves, they can pull on other people's energy and expect people to rescue and serve them. We will be discussing this type of person in chapter 4, where they show up as the victim type of energy vampire.

As middle souls, we spend about 80 percent of our time and energy trying to heal our wounds and karma that we collected in our new soul time. The people I have identified as middle souls often tell me that they feel "broken" and know that they need a lot of healing. They don't have much energy left over for helping others—and this is troubling, since they often can't find the energy to fulfill a life purpose beyond healing themselves. If you relate to being a middle soul, it's important that you honor your healing process and see that as your most important life purpose.

Once empaths grow to the point where we know with every fiber of our being that we are fully responsible for our actions and choices, we break the victim cycle once and for all and graduate to being an old soul.

Old soul is an entirely different experience that comes with its own set of new challenges. By the time we get to old soul, we have become very compassionate. Old souls are the fully evolved empaths. We know, in our very cells, that we are all connected and that we can't hurt anyone else without hurting ourselves. We feel in our bones that the planet is alive with consciousness and that all life should be revered. Reverence, love, and compassion are our normal state.

Old souls devote most of their energy to being of service to humanity. Empaths know that we are here to serve others. As old souls, the percentages are reversed: 80 percent of our energy is given to helping others and 20 percent to our own spiritual growth and evolution, which is often about healing old and unresolved karmic issues with particular people from our middle soul lifetimes. These are our soulmates, and we feel compelled to complete all of our unfinished business we have with them. Empaths are very drawn to soulmate relationships and actively seek out their soulmates for this purpose.

Look at your relationships and consider whether some of the energy vampires in your life are old soulmates of yours. Chances are good that you have an opportunity to complete your karmic cycle with them, fully empowering yourself in those relationships by setting boundaries, learning how to advocate for yourself, or walking away. Old souls still need help learning that healing others isn't about rescuing them in codependent ways, but about empowering them by setting strong and loving boundaries.

Old souls in their power know that it doesn't truly assist another soul in their growth to rescue them, just as parents know it doesn't help a child to do their homework for them. If you are an old soul, remember that no one can do another's spiritual work for them, and it only hurts both parties if you try.

Empathic old souls care more about soulmates than non-empaths do, so we easily get hooked into romantic ideals about soulmates. We long for deep intimacy and spiritual connection with others. We want our soulmate to be that idealized other who will magically read our mind and heart and meet all our needs without our having to ask. I am not saying that can't happen, but it's more likely your real soulmate is that annoying energy vampire who is pushing you to become stronger. (More about empaths and their soulmates in chapter 6.)

I share this theory of new soul, middle soul, and old soul so you can take a step back, look at the dynamic from the soul-level view, and see it as stages of spiritual evolution rather than bad people against good people.

Now that we understand the basic terrain of what it's like to be an empath, with all its challenges and all its glory, it's time to work through one of the most critical skills we all need: how to masterfully manage our emotions.

# CHAPTER 2

# Managing the Intensity of What We Feel

Being emotional is the superpower of the empath.

Our emotions are our strongest psychic power, our healing gift, the way we navigate in the world. We are old souls, and our soul speaks directly to us through our emotions, so our emotions are meant to guide us and help us relate to other people.

But being emotional is also our greatest weakness. We empaths face emotional overwhelm every day.

On our best days, we ride the waves of our emotions with skill and feel the richness of our human experience. And we follow the soul-level intuitive guidance of our emotions, allowing these feelings to steer us into a juicy life full of love and service to others.

But on our worst days, we are emotionally dysregulated, flooded, and overwhelmed, and it's worse if we have unhealed trauma in our past. We often feel like the victim of our own emotional nature.

We need to understand the impact that being an emotional mess has not only on us and our health but also on the people around us. We need to learn how to regulate our emotions. Taking care of your emotional life is just as important as taking care of your physical health, and no one else can do this for you. Being an emotional wreck and expecting other people to deal with it is not an empowering way to handle something that is really your superpower.

Let's start with one of the biggest issues for empaths: learning to distinguish between our own emotions and what we might be picking up from other people. We'll explore a few techniques that can help you tell the difference.

# What's Mine and What's Yours?

I met Taylor, a young special education teacher, in one of my workshops. She loves her job; however, the high school where she works is an environment fraught with emotional chaos. It's chock-full of stressed-out, cranky teenagers, overworked staff, and anxious parents. On top of that, because Taylor's empathic nature helps her connect with the school's most challenging, difficult students—the ones other teachers have already given up on—she often ends up with working with these students.

"I come home every day emotionally exhausted from the constant turmoil," she told me. Taylor recognized that one of the most difficult things she was dealing with as an empath was knowing which feelings were hers and which she was picking up from other people. She confessed, "I would come home with aches and pains all over, and I never could tell if any of it was actually mine."

After she learned the energy management skills we covered in the workshop and that we will also cover in this book, Taylor realized that she was picking up the emotions and physical sensations from her students. "Many of them have difficulty explaining how they are feeling, but I always knew what was going on with them." In one case, she was able to avert a medical disaster by realizing the pain she was feeling belonged to her student. It was severe enough that she put her foot down and demanded that the student be seen by the school nurse, who found a potentially catastrophic medical condition in this young man whose disabilities made it hard for him to directly communicate.

Taylor said, "I learned that I need to check in with myself every time I felt something and simply ask myself, *Is this mine or someone else's?*" She learned that she could trust the answers she found by using this simple tuning in method.

# SYSTEM CHECK MEDITATION

Do this exercise when you are feeling emotions and/or body sensations that are stronger than you normally feel, such as when you feel triggered and you are not sure if what you are feeling is yours or if it belongs to another person.

1.  Take a few breaths to center and ground yourself.

2.  Once you feel grounded, scan your body and notice any physical sensations.

3.  Direct your in-breath into the sensations with curiosity and ask yourself whether that sensation is yours or you picked it up from someone else.

4.  Either way, on your out-breath, release the energy through the soles of your feet and into the ground.

5.  Now bring your attention to your emotions and scan your emotional self. There may be a strong connection to your physical scan (we often feel our emotions as part of a physical sensation).

6.  Ask yourself, *Is this my emotion or sensation or someone else's?* The answer will come right away as a knowing, a feeling, or maybe as the word *yes* or *no*.

7.  If the emotion or sensation belongs to someone else, ask who it belongs to. It's always interesting to know, and you might see a pattern emerge.

8.  Release any lingering emotions by breathing through the soles of your feet into the ground.

9.  Now perform the same scan on your thoughts by bringing your attention to your mind. Are there any disruptive or painful thoughts? Are they yours, or did you pick them up from someone else? What do you need to do to resolve and release those thoughts?

10. Release it all on your out-breath. No matter whose sensation, feeling, or thought it is, you can release it with an acknowledgment: *Thanks for the information; now go in peace.*

With practice, you will begin to know immediately what is yours and what isn't, and you will begin to come back into equilibrium more quickly.

It's such a huge relief to be able to tell which emotions and pain are yours and which aren't. If you can release what isn't yours, then you are on your way to drastically reducing the emotional overwhelm that empaths suffer from.

What remains is learning how to effectively handle your own emotions. Let's start by taking a look at three of the most difficult emotional issues that empaths deal with.

## Anxiety, Depression, and Addictions

Anxiety is so common for empaths that for many of us it is a constant companion. The lack of adequate boundaries gives us a feeling of raw, exposed nerves that leads to our feeling unsafe in the world. It is as if we were born anxious.

Many factors can create anxiety in an empath. The first is our porous, spongy nature; it's simply difficult to be a part of the world when we feel everything so deeply and so easily. Being a psychic sponge makes us vulnerable. And, sadly, I notice that empaths are more frequently targeted for bullying and abuse than other people are. An aggressive person looking for a target will often choose to pick on a softhearted, nonviolent empath who doesn't have a strong natural boundary.

Another cause for anxiety is the lack of emotional and energetic coherence in the people around us. From our earliest years, as empathic children, it's critical that we be around people who are consistent in what they say and what they do—people who are genuine in their emotions and their energy. Unfortunately, many of us grow up in families where the spoken words do not match the felt reality. Empaths can relax and live without anxiety when we are around people who have this energetic and emotional consistency—what you feel is what you get.

Moira is a gentle-hearted young woman who walks dogs for a living. She says, "People are a big problem for me. I hate it when they don't say what they are really feeling. I can feel when people aren't fine even when they say that they are. Animals aren't like that; their energy is pure, and they don't lie." An empath can spot mismatched energy in people a mile away—that is, when people who say one thing but their emptions and energy convey something completely different.

Moira told me that being outside all the time is very grounding for her. "I get to be away from the light and the noise too." Moira has a sensitivity to fluorescent lights and WiFi. "I remember feeling anxious leaving my house as a child, unless I was going outside. The woods were a safety zone for me," she explained. "Other people's houses always felt so weird, and full of creepy and sad energy. Sleepovers made me anxious as a child. In fact, I always had background anxiety; I just never knew when some yucky energy would be waiting around the next corner."

Moira said that she has a very limited ability to be in the world, living in the anxious, hypervigilant state she had become accustomed to. But as she has learned how to manage her energy, she has been able to take bigger risks and not narrow her life down to being outside only with dogs.

Fortunately, as empaths get better at energy management, setting effective boundaries, and processing their own emotions, our anxiety levels go way down.

Many empaths also suffer from depression. Again, there are many contributing factors, and we must explore each case individually to find the root cause of someone's depression. This could be unhealed past trauma or the isolation that social anxiety brings. Depression also may stem from strong emotional states, like anger and grief, that we have turned inward on ourselves. And I see many empaths who feel depression when they can't figure out how to be a part of the world and fully step into their life purpose.

There is a horrible catch-22 for empaths. We need to be around people to live our life purpose, yet that puts us right in the line of fire, going into chaotic environments with people who need our help.

Any unprocessed emotions can clog up an empath and create depression. Add to that toxic stew the heavy burden of other people's pain and suffering, and you may have empathic overload. If we spend a lot of time around chronically negative people, we will absorb their pain, anger, and misery to the point that it bogs us down too. Our psychic sponge is full of other people's gunk, and if we don't know how to clear it, we are vulnerable to depression.

Healing from depression is a path unique to each of us; there is no "one size fits all" cure. But it is extremely important to seek help. Depression is nothing to be ashamed of. Tell someone how you are feeling, and seek counseling.

We empaths often fall victim to addictions. Addiction is a way for empaths and non-empaths alike to turn off troublesome feelings, and because we deal with so much emotion—our own and others'—we have a stronger likelihood than non-empaths do of becoming addicted. In addition to the more classic substance addictions of alcohol, drugs, and tobacco, we can become addicted to anything from games on our smartphones to shopping to social media.

Empaths use our addictions to stop our own feelings, to numb ourselves to other people's feelings, and to muffle the general oversensitivity to life that we suffer from. Our addictive choices bring temporary relief, but at a huge price.

# HELP FOR ANXIETY, DEPRESSION, AND ADDICTIONS

If you are struggling with these challenges, it's critical to get help and healing for yourself. There's no need to suffer, as there are many effective healing methods and treatments for this type of emotional pain:

- Get counseling. It really does work, especially if you find a therapist whom you connect with. Look for someone who has specific experience in whatever you are dealing with.

- Take medication, if a professional determines it could help you. If you can't function, meds can really help you get your feet under you so that you can do the things you need to do.

- Seek help from healers. Many empaths respond very well to energy medicine techniques like Reiki, homeopathy, bodywork, and acupuncture.

- Find a tribe. Go to a support group. Connect with AA or Al-Anon. Join a meditation, yoga, or Reiki class and find the other sensitive and magical people in your area.

- Spend time in nature. There is a deep healing and energy clearing when we connect with nature. No matter the weather, try to get out and take a walk every day—aim for thirty minutes, and more is better.

- Choose a healthy lifestyle. Eating clean and getting some vigorous exercise and plentiful sleep makes a huge difference. If you need help, get support with stocking your kitchen and learning new eating habits; and find a walking partner or gym buddy or trainer.

- Find spiritual support, whatever you resonate with. Go to church, temple, or mosque. Find a meditation class, or learn a body-centered practice like yoga or tai chi. Even fifteen minutes of daily meditation with a meditation app on your phone can have a huge positive impact on your mental health.

I have seen many empaths with addiction issues get a leg up in the recovery process by learning better ways to manage their boundaries and their energy. Recovery is a difficult process that takes a lot of dedication and hard work, but I have seen some miracles happen when addicted empaths learn the energy management practices that we will discover in chapter 3.

There is no shame in getting help with your mental and emotional health—in fact, it's critical. I don't know anyone who can work through their deeper emotional issues on their own. Therapists, energy healers, and bodyworkers can and should be your allies here.

Now that we have steadied our mental health, let's take a look at learning how to manage our own emotional states.

## Repressing Our Feelings

I remember being a young child and getting teased and bullied at school. I have a very distinct memory of being in the lunch room and swearing to myself that I wasn't going to cry in front of my tormentors. It felt like I was swallowing a huge lump of energy, like a hot knife in my throat or maybe like trying to swallow an entire apple at once. And then there was a burning feeling in my gut, like a coal of anger and shame smoldering in my belly. It became a familiar practice, as I swallowed my feelings this way. It came with physical issues, too, as I suffered from acid reflux and dodgy digestion. I had learned a classic way to repress my emotions. This lasted until I was in my twenties, when I went to therapy and learned a more productive way to process them.

Repressing your feelings is a pattern that forms in childhood. To live a healthy emotional life, we must address and resolve this response. Empathic children are very sensitive; we can cry at the drop of a hat, we have emotional meltdowns easily, and we are usually considerably more anxious than other children. And most of us quickly learn that our parents cannot deal with our being overly emotional. Each family has its own unspoken rules about how emotional you are allowed to be, as well which emotions are accepted and which are not. And each family system has its own way of teaching emotional repression to their children.

Darius, a young Reiki student of mine, told me this story: "In my house, it wasn't okay to have feelings, especially for boys. Boys are supposed to be tough, and my dad would threaten me when I cried, even when I was really young. It was along the lines of 'Stop crying and whining or I will really give you something to cry about!' That was a message that I heard over and over again."

Darius knew that his anxiety and sadness made his father uncomfortable and overwhelmed.

*When I was five years old, my mother got cancer and was sick for a long time. She was my emotional connection and understood me, while my dad was overwhelmed with working and taking care of us kids. He couldn't stand it when I cried or had any feelings at all, which was tough, because it was a difficult and sad situation. I knew even when I was five that he was at the end of his rope and that I had to take care of him or he was going to crack and then we would all be in big trouble. I learned how to suck it all up and repress my feelings. I never cried or whined on the outside. I hid it all so I wouldn't upset my mom and dad. I also became everyone's caretaker and took care of my brothers and sister even at that young age. I would be sick, have a panic attack or a nightmare about once a week.*

Darius had learned the trick that many empaths resort to for survival: to run all his emotional energy through his body. He would deny and repress his feelings until they burst out in physical symptoms such as irritable bowel syndrome. But as he got older and went to therapy and learned Reiki, he acquired some healthier ways to release all the feelings that he had been stuffing inside.

Clearly, when we have such unhealthy patterns, we need to examine and work through them. Let's start by looking at how you might be repressing your emotions. Chances are very good that you've inherited a family pattern, so think about what has always happened in your family when someone gets emotional. Here are some common ways that we repress our emotions.

- Holding your breath and using your willpower to push them down.

- Dissociating and getting lost in imaginary worlds of pretend and fantasy, like reading romance novels or binge-watching TV shows.

- Getting busy and doing practical things to get them off your checklist. If you *do, do, do* then you don't have to *feel, feel, feel.*

- Forgetting about your own emotions and experiences by constantly taking care of other people.

- Using addictions like food, smoking, and alcohol to numb your emotions.

- Starting trouble with others to distract yourself with a good fight. Battles with neighbors or coworkers, road rage, or getting overheated at sports games prevent us from looking inward.

There are countless other ways that you can learn to push your feelings aside, but these are some of the most common patterns. What happens when you are basically a sensitive person who is full of all the feels, and you push them all down? Eventually, they are going to explode out of you in a painful process that we call *flooding.*

# Emotional Flooding

We can push down our emotions for only so long before they burst out of us. This is flooding, and it's no fun at all. When we flood, it feels terrible. It's scary, overwhelming, and exhausting, and it's very hard on the people around us too. Ironically, flooding can feel so horrible that it can lead to even more repressing in a vicious cycle. I have heard many empaths say, "I can't cry, because if I do, it feels like I will never stop." The fear of flooding actually leads to more repressing.

When someone has a recurring pattern of repressing and then flooding, we tend to tiptoe around them, never knowing when the flood might come.

Here are some common ways that empaths can flood:

- Emotional meltdowns, like crying or rage storms. This can be puddling into tears or having a temper tantrum, but to an extreme where you can't stop.

- Emotional hysteria, which can be grief and anxiety all mixed together, coming out in an explosive way.

- "Nervous" stomach and GI upsets like vomiting or diarrhea, which can become hardwired into us as irritable bowel syndrome and other recurring gastric upset.

- Migraines. We release the emotional energy as pain and sometimes vomiting.

- Anxiety overloads, like panic attacks.

- Self-harming, like overeating or restricted eating, cutting, promiscuity, and other risky and addictive behaviors.

My super-soft empath friend Nancy told me this story:

*I started getting migraines when I was really young. Whenever I got sad, I would want to cry, but it upset my mother too much. She told me once that she felt like she was a bad mother every time I cried, so I had to smile all the time, even when I was sad. But when all the sadness would build up too much, I would get a migraine. It was the only time my mother was nice to me and nurturing. I would have to go into a dark room, and she would sit with me and put a cold cloth on my head. The migraines could last a day or two, and I would feel sort of washed clean after them.*

Nancy carried those migraines into her adult life and could accurately predict when she was going to get one. "I would always get a migraine after something stressful or emotional happened in my life, until I learned that I needed to write about my feelings in my journal every day and cry when I needed to. If I took care to let myself have my feelings every day, then no more migraines."

When we are working through our emotions, it's important to remember that there are no bad or wrong ones. There are unhealthy ways to express emotions, which we learn mostly from our family. And there are the emotions that your family deemed were "bad" and that good people should never express. Some families allow angry arguing and yelling but no crying, ever. In other families, members cry easily but it's considered disrespectful to show any anger.

Many of us have promised ourselves that we'll never behave as badly as our parents did: *I swear I'll never fly into rages and be violent like Dad.* Then you repress any anger that you feel.

Anger is a perfectly good and useful emotion, a natural response when something is not fair or we need to set a better boundary with someone. Anger serves us well when its force empowers us, setting us in motion—for example, to say no to something. We need this empowering force, but we have learned destructive ways to express it that really aren't okay. We need to find a way to move the energy out of our body without harming ourselves or others.

Here are a few things to keep in mind as we strive to have a healthy emotional life:

- There are no "bad" feelings; they all give us important information about ourselves. But there are ways of expressing our feelings that can hurt ourselves and others.

- The goal is to move the emotional energy out of our bodies without impacting ourself or others.

- We are responsible for our own feelings; no one can "make" us feel anything. We are also fully responsible for how we express them.

- It's not okay to beat yourself up for your feelings, to tell yourself that you are bad or wrong for feeling something, or to target yourself in any way.

- It's also not okay to punish or manipulate others with our feelings or use them as an excuse to hurt others—the classic "It's your fault that you made me so mad; that's why I yelled at you." We must learn to own it all.

Take note of where you are on the spectrum of emotional repressing and flooding. Do you repress, repress, and then flood? Or are you a constant flooder? Or do you repress your emotions at work and then flood all over your poor family when you get home? You can learn a lot about your emotional processing patterns if you observe yourself, and maybe journal about it. Once you see your patterns, you can work on regulating and expressing your emotions in a more healthy and productive manner.

# Learning to Contain Our Emotional Intensity

Repressing and flooding are two ends of the emotional pendulum swing; the healthy middle ground is called *containing*. Containing means allowing ourselves to fully feel all our emotions, neither repressing them nor acting out and behaving badly. We use a breathing technique to fully allow the feeling energy to move through us, without acting it out in any way. This allows our emotional energy to flow through our system in a natural way.

When we feel an emotion rising and allow it to bubble up naturally, it sweeps through our whole system, often in an energy pattern that starts at our feet and washes up our spine. When we let the emotion move through us unimpeded, for normal everyday emotions, it's gone in a minute or two. Of course we all go through periods of more extreme emotions, which are also perfectly normal to feel, like grief at a loss or anger at abuse. Whichever one we are dealing with, when we try to hold it back and repress it, it sticks around, muddies up our system, and creates problems. Have you ever noticed that if you let yourself cry when you are sad, it may pass in a few minutes, but if you suck it up and repress it, you feel sad for hours?

Watch very young children as they handle their feelings. In many everyday cases they have the feeling, get it all out by crying, screaming or laughing, and then it's over and they are on to the next one. It helps to retain that kind of emotional fluidity into adulthood.

Let's try it out.

# BREATHING TO CONTAIN
# YOUR EMOTIONS

You can do this anywhere, anytime. I do think it's useful to have your feet on the ground to help you stay grounded, but I have done it lying in bed and even while I was driving. Use it when you feel the wave of an emotion coming on, or when you feel tightness in your body that you suspect is a stuck and repressed emotion.

1. Push your feet into the ground to help you ground yourself, and take a deep breath into your belly.

2. Scan your body and see if the emotions are coming from a part of your body, like your heart or your belly.

3. Breath up from the bottom of your feet, directing the breath to the part of your body where the feeling is. If the feeling is in your belly, breath into your belly and exhale out the top of your head.

4. Allow the emotions to come up with each breath. You are not going to say or do anything, just breathe and observe. Lean into it and see how much of the emotion you can allow yourself to feel.

5. Stay curious and see if you can track the emotion back to whatever triggered you. Curiosity keeps us out of self-judgment. If the emotion gets intense, breathe a little deeper.

6. Try putting your hand on your heart or your belly and flow some compassion out to yourself.

7. When the emotion fully moves through your body, you can relax and go back to your normal breathing.

Practicing this exercise teaches us how to lean into the emotion and let it pass through us without harming ourselves or other people in the process. It lets us fully feel all our feels without the painful pattern of repressing and flooding. As super-powerful and effective as it is, however, we empaths need additional ways to help us maintain and master our emotional superpowers.

## Counseling

If you have never worked with a counselor before, I highly recommend that you try it. It's a fantastic way to learn many skills that empaths need, including how to gain perspective about our emotions and how to express them in a healthy manner. And counseling is vital in clearing up past trauma, so if you have unresolved traumas, this is a must for you.

Take your time finding a therapist who resonates with you. It's okay to try as many of them as you need to before you click with someone. I highly recommend therapists who use a somatic approach in their work. They will help you connect your emotions with your body, which helps you avoid overthinking and intellectualizing your emotions.

## Emotional Freedom Technique

Many people find the emotional freedom technique (EFT), also called *tapping*, very useful, particularly with relieving anxiety. We learn to tap with our fingers on different points on the body while connecting to our feelings. These points lie on the bladder meridian, which holds the emotional charge in our energy system. As we tap those points while expressing our emotions, it releases stuck emotional energy. It's very easy to learn and highly effective.

There are hundreds of free tapping videos on YouTube on any subject you can think of. You can use tapping during times when you are having an emotional upset and can't find anyone to talk to about it. Tapping has been researched and used with veterans to relieve their stress and anxiety; the beneficial changes are often permanent.

## Journaling

Journaling your emotions is also a good way to process them, moving them out of the body and expressing them in a healthy way that doesn't negatively impact you or anyone else. Let all those emotions out in writing, and the journal becomes a container for them. If you're concerned that others might find your journal, try writing in a password-protected file on your laptop or computer.

It's a simple, cost-effective, and powerful way to process and honor your emotions daily, or as often as you need to. If you are prone to repressing your emotions, journaling can help you open to your feelings. Repressors often feel things better in hindsight, so it's fine to think about it that way. People who are used to repressing their emotions don't always notice their feelings in the moment and may realize that they'd had a feeling only much later. With time and journal work, repressors can learn to experience their emotions in the moment. Maybe you write in your journal, "Yesterday I got really mad at my boss!" Over time, you can see the patterns in your journal and work out the whys. "I notice that I always get angry when I feel disrespected and unappreciated."

Flooders deeply benefit by learning to flood in the pages of their journal. In your journal, you can flood away with impunity and get it all off your chest and out of your body. It's nice and safe there. And the people in your life will appreciate your finding a better alternative to flooding onto them.

# Meditation

We empaths, even more so than non-empaths, need to develop a daily meditation practice to process our emotions, a practice we can rely on throughout life. Meditation is good for your entire being, from stress reduction to learning to connect with more universal energies. And it is also very good at helping you learn to manage your emotional life, especially in finding a healthy way to stop over identifying with your emotions.

Most meditative practices are *concentration meditation* practices. These work by focusing your concentration on something like your breath or a mantra with the instruction that you label your thoughts and feelings as such. This helps you learn to let them slide by without attaching too much importance to them.

This kind of meditation is a great practice for people who feel overly identified with their emotions; it helps put them in perspective, to realize that we have feelings and thoughts, and we are also more than that.

A different practice, *insight meditation*, does the opposite; it teaches us to deeply examine every emotion and body sensation, looking for self-understanding. It's a powerful practice for people who have learned to numb their emotions and don't feel anything.

For either practice, I encourage you to seek out a teacher or a group to help support you while you are learning; it will be much easier and more effective than trying to learn and master them on your own.

I recommend trying each on for size to see which resonates for you. Adding it to your daily self-care routine will help keep your emotional channels clear so they don't back up and lead to the unhealthy repress-and-flood pattern.

It is our responsibility as empaths to choose a higher emotional state for ourselves. We are the emoters in this world; we set and hold the emotional frequencies here. When we are filled with painful, low-vibration emotions—like hatred, shame, fear, and guilt—we bring more of those frequencies to the planet and hold them. When we become the masters of our own emotions, we can choose in every moment to feel joy, love, and peace—and when we do, we uplift ourselves, others, and the world itself.

Choosing the higher-vibration emotions also helps heal other people. I guarantee that when you flood, it has a painful effect on the people around you, too.

When we feel stuck emotions, we can use our tools to release and express those feelings quickly and easily and so return to a higher emotional vibration. As we do this, we heal ourselves and those around us. Your emotions are your superpower, your biggest gift to the world. Use them wisely.

Now that we have learned to manage our own energy field and our emotions, we are ready to learn how to really set boundaries. In the next chapter, we'll learn what a boundary really is, as well as how to set powerful ones in even the most difficult situations.

# CHAPTER 3

# Learning to Protect Our Energy

Minji is a beautiful young empath who works as a hair stylist. She came to me looking for help for managing her energy in the chaos of a busy salon in downtown Boston.

> I have my hands on people all day, and the salon is full of people talking, loud music, and drama. I love the creative aspect of my job, but the empathic overload is killing me. If I don't learn how to manage my energy in this environment, I am going to have to quit. I am so tired when I come home that I can't do anything else, and recently my husband told me that I am no fun anymore. It's true. I just want to sleep when I get home, and I have dropped all my hobbies and most of my friends. We want to have kids, but I think that would throw me over the edge. My sensitivity is putting a strain on my marriage. I need help!

It's an important issue for all of us empaths. We need and want to be a part of the world, yet until we learn some practical ways to manage our energy, we are at the mercy of our own sensitivity.

The good news is that there are two powerful ways to manage our energy. First, we'll learn about the human energy field and why it's important to empaths. Then we'll examine some tools and techniques that will help you master your emotional life rather than being a slave to it. Once we have learned how to manage our energy at these two levels, many of the painful parts of being an empath—like empathic overload, depression, and anxiety—resolve themselves.

Let's get started.

# The Human Energy Field

Energy medicine practitioners have long known about the human energy field. Writings and teaching on this topic go back thousands of years, all the way to the yoga sutras and Chinese medicine teaching. Anyone who has practiced or received energy medicine techniques like acupuncture and Reiki has probably experienced their own energy field, and now scientists have proved its existence.

It's important to understand this part of us, because the energy field of an empath is different from that of non-empathic people. And learning to strengthen our energy field is one of the quickest and most efficient ways to live more powerfully in the world. Let's explore all the different parts of your energy field.

## Parts of the Energy Field

Many traditional healing approaches, chiefly those arising in Eastern belief systems, describe this invisible, energetic part of us existing beyond our physical body. This energy, which exists both around and in us, is made up of a few different complex, interconnected systems:

- The aura, which is made up of layers of energy that extend three-dimensionally away from your body to about arm's length.

- The chakra system: seven primary energy centers that regulate your physical body, your emotions, your sense of self, your relationships, your voice, your mind, and your connection to cosmic consciousness.

- The life purpose line, also called the *hara line*. This energetic structure occupies the same physical space as your spine, and your chakras connect into it. As the name suggests, this part of your energy field gives you direction about your life purpose.

- The grounding cord, which connects your whole being to the earth.

- The energy meridian system, used by many energy medicine practitioners, such as acupuncturists.

Learning to recognize and work with your energy field can help you to stay grounded, reduce empathic overload, and clear the unwanted energy that you pick up from others.

Looking at the human energy field is a fantastic way to understand a few important things about being an empath. Because I have been an energy medicine practitioner for so many years, I have perceived the energy fields of many different people. I've noticed that an empath has a slightly different energy field from a non-empathic person, and those differences are part of why empaths can become energetically and emotionally overwhelmed.

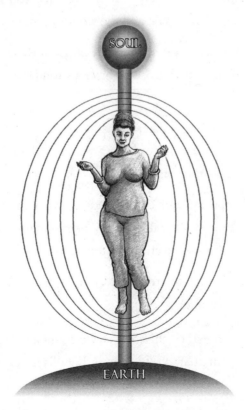

As I've helped empaths change and repair their energy fields, especially the aura, their experience of the world has changed too. They've felt safer, less anxious and overwhelmed, and more powerful and grounded. Changing your energy field is like changing a habit; it takes some patience and dedication to do it, but it yields powerful results.

We are going to be working a lot with your aura—the part of your energy field that extends beyond your body. Of its seven layers, the most important for empaths is the boundary layer. Visualize the aura as a bubble that extends around you: the boundary layer is the outer skin of the bubble.

## Your Energetic Boundary

The boundary layer of your aura is important. When it's strong, you have a good boundary between yourself and the world. It's like your skin, keeping you on the inside and the world on the outside.

- The boundary layer of the aura protects each of us from the world. Non-empathic people have a strong layer; empaths have a spongy layer.

- Physical and emotional trauma can rip holes in your boundary layer, making it weaker, so you are more vulnerable to energetic and psychic invasion.

- This boundary layer corresponds to your immune system, so when it's weak, you will have a weaker immune system and also more sensitivities to chemical toxins and EMF radiation.

- Habitual and addictive drinking and drugs also weaken this layer of your aura.

Learning to strengthen this layer is like changing a habit, but it has huge payoffs in your stamina, health, and ability to cope with people and the world.

The biggest difference between the energy field of an empath and a non-empath is that the empath's is usually more expanded and diffuse. This means that an empath's aura is much wider, sometimes twice as wide as that of a non-empathic person. And the boundary layer of an empath is porous like a sponge, creating a diffuse quality.

Empaths are psychic sponges, so there is less of a boundary between an empath, other people, and the world itself. To empaths, this can feel like *I don't know where I end and the world begins!* This expanded, spongy energy field makes it easy for us to merge with others and the world; our deep desire for empathy also drives this urge to merge.

A non-empathic person's energy field is more like a solid bubble, with a substantial barrier on the outside like an eggshell. This makes non-empathic people much more resilient and tougher in difficult situations. Funky energy will roll off their backs without directly impacting them.

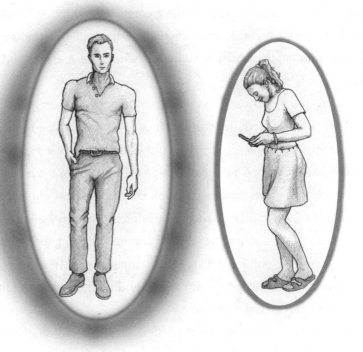

The spongy, expanded quality of the empath's energy field also means that when you go into a group, your aura expands, so all the people in the room are actually inside your aura. A non-empathic person can be in the same group, but they feel completely distinct, separated, and individuated from the group. They are safe, secure, and alone inside their bubble in a way that we empaths are not.

Let's imagine that an empath and non-empath go to the movies together. As they sit down, the empath's aura expands to occupy a big space in the theater, including all the people sitting in that space, so all those people are now inside the empath's aura. Meanwhile, the non-empath is safe and comfy in their bubble all by themselves.

Once the movie starts and everyone in the theater has the same strong emotions all at the same time, the empath will quickly hit empathic overload. The empath is trying to manage their own feelings, plus being flooded with everyone else's emotions, especially the adjacent people who are sitting inside their aura. The empath leaves the movie emotionally exhausted, their energetic sponge fully saturated, while the non-empathic friend actually enjoys all the emotional and visual stimulation, which is really fun when you are safe and secure inside your own bubble.

This spongy aura can be a powerfully adaptive strategy for empathic children who grow up in an uncertain and unpredictable household. If you are an empathic child in an alcoholic family, for example, that spongy, expanded energy field allows you to sense what is happening with your parents as a safety measure. Even a two-year-old empath will expand his aura to include the whole house. That way he knows where everyone is in the house and whether Mommy is in a good or bad place today. Empathic children will use their empathic abilities to diagnose in an instant how their parents are feeling and then adapt to the situation to try and caretake their parents.

Learning to contract the expanded aura in a crowded situation is very important; mastering this skill will help tremendously to minimize empathic overload. And changing the habit of having a sponge instead of a bubble is also key. We will learn how to do this, using a visualization and breathing technique that can be done anywhere and any time. The aura responds very well to our imagination, and we can actually control and reprogram this part of ourselves.

## CREATING A PROTECTIVE BUBBLE

1.  Stand or sit with your feet on the floor and your arms and legs uncrossed (which creates a better energy flow through your system).

2.  Take a deep breath into the center of your belly, and on your exhale imagine you are releasing any extra energy you are carrying.

3.  Now imagine that you can sense the outer skin of your energy field. You may see it, feel it, or just know where it is. If it is beyond an arm's length, pull it in toward your body so it is about at arm's length.

4.  Now imagine that it is made of something more solid than a sponge. Maybe an eggshell, a crystal ball, or a big rubber ball. Use whatever image works for you.

5.  Declare that this boundary layer is going to let in energy that is supportive for you and keep out unsupportive energy. Nothing crosses this boundary without your permission.

Use this technique when you need to be somewhere that would typically send you into empathic overload, like a movie theater, crowded restaurant, or shopping mall. When you are home alone or out in nature you can release this and let your aura expand as far and wide as you want.

The most important point of this exercise is to change our energetic habit of having a spongy, porous boundary layer. With practice, we can change the sponge into something more solid, more permanent.

This boundary layer ideally is like a cell membrane—semi-permeable, allowing in what is nurturing to us and keeping out what isn't. Without this protective layer, our energy leaks out easily, leaving us exhausted and drained of energy; then, like a wrung-out sponge, we soak up all kinds of energy around us. This leaking and sponging up is the cause of much of the empathic overload that we experience. It's important to the discussion of energy training, because our psychic ability can be a source of energy leaks that involve powerful energetic and psychic connections that empaths often form with other people.

For example, having a weak boundary layer means that it's very easy to get drained when an energy vampire is around. It can feel as if the energy vampire sticks a straw into you and takes a big suck on that straw.

Energy vampires can latch onto us to drain us in a few different ways. I see an *energy cord* or a *hook* that connects the energy vampire to their energetic supply person. Cords and hooks are invisible energetic connections that we form with other people. When we're dealing with an energy vampire, cords most frequently go into the energy center in our solar plexus—the one governing power and self-esteem. An energy vampire will try to hook you with an energy cord to that center to dominate your will and control you. You might notice that when you are around certain people, you instinctively cover this part of your belly with your arms.

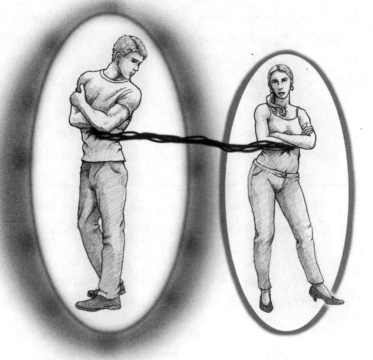

Energy vampires can also hook us by looking us in the eye, so if you are around someone who vamps you, avoid looking directly into their eyes. We can also avoid these hooks by not engaging in direct conversation with them. Try nodding or saying something very neutral like "hmmm" instead. Here are some powerful techniques to avoid these common draining tactics.

# THE ENERGY CLOSED POSITION

Using these techniques closes all the openings in your energy field and makes it harder for someone to hook you with an energy cord. You can do it quite discreetly even in the middle of a social event. I did it once when I was on TV!

1.  Start with the bubble exercise. You can cut to the chase by quickly imagining that your bubble is up around you and your aura is secured at arm's length around you.

2.  Stand or sit with your feet parallel, big toes next to each other. Close your knees and thighs too, as much as you can.

3.  Fold your arms across your solar plexus to cover this part of you, as it is extra vulnerable.

4.  Touch your tongue to the roof of your mouth; this closes and locks down many of the energy meridians.

5.  If you are talking to someone, don't look them in the eye. Look at their eyebrow or the bridge of their nose. It will seem as if you are looking at them, not avoiding eye contact, so it passes as polite.

6.  Don't engage in conversation. Reply as neutrally as possible: "Oh, really?" "Is that so?" "How interesting..."

7.  Breath slowly in a long, four-count breath and keep the energy moving up and down your spine with your breath.

This is very useful when dealing with energy vampires you can't get away from. It will pass in society as polite and normal, so it's good with bosses and relatives, but it provides no energetic opening for someone to hook you with. On the other hand, if you *do* want to invite intimacy with someone, looking them in the eye, sitting down with your feet and legs more open, and a relaxed body posture all will create an open energy field that your acquaintance can hook into. Just make a clear choice.

Now that you have a good basic knowledge of the empath's energy field, let's get to the basics of how to manage your energy in a way that both strengthens and empowers you.

## The Art of Grounding

Grounding is a word that we commonly use, but what does it really mean? We can break it down into three major aspects:

- Being in your body

- Being connected to the earth

- Being in the present moment

We have all had those moments of being ungrounded, which can lead to undesirable outcomes, like leaving your briefcase or your cup of coffee on the roof of your car and driving off, losing track of your wallet and key, or walking into a room and stopping to wonder why you walked in there.

Empaths can have a false sense of security about being ungrounded, thinking that it feels safer because it's numbing to dissociate. But you are much more at risk if you are dissociated, and therefore ungrounded. If you are out of your body, you are at risk of being targeted by an energy vampire and absorbing unwanted energies of all kinds.

Your real power comes from being fully embodied. And I mean all of your power—your personal and spiritual mojo as well as a powerful connection to your intuition and psychic abilities. Your body is wise; it is much more tuned in to what's happening around you than your mind is, and you will miss all that wisdom if you are dissociated.

Sadly, we empaths often have a bad habit of being more out than in, especially if we have had trauma in our past. It's a normal reaction to dissociate when a trauma is occurring. If that has happened to you, it's another reason to spend more time cleaning up your trauma.

So how do we become more grounded? If you are habitually ungrounded, it takes just that: changing a habit. I love a mixture of guided meditations and breathing practices as well as very practical things that we can do daily. Let's talk about those first.

## Grounding Practices

Sometimes very practical methods are the best way to ground. Try these and see what works for you.

- Any kind of exercise, especially heavy exercise like weightlifting and running, but even a brisk walk will work.

- Doing practical tasks like cooking, doing the dishes, housecleaning, and weeding the garden. Do it with your full presence and the intention to ground yourself.

- Eating and drinking. Pay attention and do mindful eating. It can be helpful to choose energetically denser foods like proteins or healthy, whole-grain carbs. Watch out for mood-changers like sugar, caffeine, and alcohol; they can ground us but also can have a negative health impact and stimulate addiction.

- Stay hydrated and make sure you have enough minerals and electrolytes in your diet. When I feel ungrounded, I put a little Himalayan salt in my water.

- Put your bare feet on the ground. I keep a big river rock under my desk, and I put my bare feet on it when I am writing. Rubber-soled shoes disrupt our connection to the earth's energy frequency, but standing in the grass or even on concrete reconnects us. "Earthing" shoes and mats can help.

- Being outside in nature is helpful. Hug a tree; sit on the ground and breathe deeply.

These are good starting points. Try the ones that appeal, and find out what works for you. There are many ways to ground yourself; the important thing is to be consistent with it. Make sure you catch yourself when you are ungrounded and do something about it.

Here is another good way to ground using a meditation and breath practice. You'll use your attention and breath to connect with the earth using the part your energy field called the grounding cord. This is like the root of a tree that runs down from your tailbone through your legs and extends into the ground. Like other parts of our energy field, it responds very well to our visualization and imagination, so we can imagine that it's going down through the earth and connecting our body to the earth.

I use this in healing sessions when I need to be more grounded and hold space for my clients or when I am out in the world and become ungrounded. I did this while I was writing this section in Starbucks today, or I never would have made it through this chapter!

Let's try it out now.

# GROUNDING CORD MEDITATION

Begin by sitting with your feet on the floor, arms and legs uncrossed. You can also do this standing up.

1.  Take a deep breath into your belly and become aware of your bones. Your bones are the most grounded part of your body, since they are dense and solid.

2.  Breath light through the top of your head and down into your belly. On the exhale, imagine that your spine is extending from your tailbone like the big tap root of a tree.

3.  With every inhale, breath light into the top of your head, and with every exhale imagine that the grounding cord is going down through all the layers of the building you are in and down through all the layers of the ground.

4.  Get it as far down into the ground as you can, and make it nice and wide, maybe trashcan wide or sewer pipe wide.

5.  You may feel heaviness or tingling in your legs and tailbone as you do this. This is a sign that it's working.

Practice this exercise whenever you notice you are out of your body. Over time, you will become more permanently grounded.

Now that we have learned to keep ourselves grounded, the next foundational energy management practice is clearing all the unwanted energy we pick up from sponging.

# Energetic Clearing

Clearing is how we release the energy that we pick up from our environment and other people. As I've said, we empaths tend to be energetic sponges, and we need to regularly wring out that sponge to clear three different types of energy:

- Our own overflow of emotions

- The energy, emotions, and physical symptoms that we sponge up from other people

- The leftover energy of the environments that we inhabit

Clearing should be done at least daily, more often whenever needed, like whenever you feel the symptoms of empathic overload. I recommend an evening practice of clearing. Add it to your before-bed routine, and you will sleep better without the energetic residue of the day lingering in your system. You might also want to do a clearing after you leave work and before you get home, or after you have been in an energetically stressful environment like a hospital or big-box store. And definitely after any interactions with people that leave you feeling drained or flustered.

# Clearing Practices

These are useful and practical clearing practices that you can easily incorporate into your daily routine. Salt, water, and breathing techniques are the backbone of these practices.

## Using Salt

Salt is a super purifier. Its ability to clear energy has made its use in clearing practices a staple worldwide. Part of what makes it so powerful is its crystalline structure and chemical and energetic properties, which make it a powerful purificant.

- Use a salt scrub in your shower as needed. I make my own with table salt and essential oils, like frankincense and myrrh, which also have clearing powers. Peppermint and lavender are also potent clearing oils. You can also make it fancy with sea salt or pink Himalayan salt. Rub the salt scrub all over your skin and imagine that anything you've picked up is going down the drain.

- Do a salt bath by adding salt to your bath water. I take a salt tub before bed, especially if I have done a lot of psychic work. Any kind of salt is fine; I tend to like less refined salts, like sea salt or Epsom salt (which is not an edible salt, but a pharmaceutical preparation of magnesium, sulfur, and oxygen). Add in essential oils or anything else that makes the bath appealing. I have been known to add holy water to my tub on really tough days.

- It's said that salt around your bed and in the corners of your room at night will keep away psychic stalkers, especially in a room that has funky energy.

- I use a bowl of salt under my massage table in my office to clear energy from my clients, and change the salt weekly.

- A salt lamp is a must-have for sensitive children and makes a great night light for children who are disturbed by nightmares or nighttime visits from spirits.

## Using Water

Water is also a great purifier, not only in the expected way of washing things. Water can hold energy and change its form and structure depending on the emotions and thoughts of people around the water as Dr. Masaru Emoto professed to find in experiments, detailed in his book *The Hidden Messages in Water*.[3]

According to Emoto, water responds to our intentions, so when you are in the shower, imagine that all the energy that does not belong to you is washing out and heading down the drain. Soaking in a tub will also clear energy—especially if you add some salt, as just discussed.

Try washing your hands with intention. I have done this everywhere, even in airport bathrooms, with great effect. I prefer cold or cool water for this. Use your intention and say this affirmation as you wash your hands: "May this water release all that does not resonate with me, all that is not mine, and anything that is mine that I am ready to release."

Even being near water is clearing, which is one reason why we flock to lakes, oceans, and rivers when we can on our vacations. Being near running water is especially restorative. Getting into the water is even better, and the salt water of the ocean is a fantastic way to clear your energy.

Blessed and holy water is revered by many as a very powerful substance. Because water holds our intentions so powerfully, blessed water is extra powerful for clearing. Almost all religions and faith traditions have a water blessing ceremony, and you can get holy water from almost all churches. Add a tiny bit of it to your bath, or drink it. I always have holy or blessed water in my office, and sometimes I carry it in my purse.

It's very easy to make your own blessed water. Here is a simple but powerful water ritual that you can do with a glass or bottle of water anytime.

# SIMPLE WATER BLESSING EXERCISE

1. Get a glass or bottle of water. Any kind will do.

2. Hold the glass in your hand and set your intention to clear and purify the water. Imagine that your hands are sending energy to the water. You can say something like "I purify and bless this water." Call on a higher power if you like: "In the name of God/Jesus/Mary/Buddha/Allah." Or pray your favorite prayer while you are holding the water.

3. You can also hold the water near your heart and imagine that your own heart energy and love are going into the water.

4. Now sip the water with the intention that the water will clear, purify, and nourish you with that blessed energy from the inside out. Know that this water is going into every cell in your body and bringing the blessing with you.

5. As you drink, you can say in your mind *May I receive the blessings of this water. May it clear, purify, and nourish me for my highest good.*

6. You can add many other energies to creating blessed water. Try leaving water out on the night of a full moon or in the sun to charge the water. You can also add crystals, herbs, and even some essential oils to make super-charged blessed water.

## Using Your Breath

Breathing is also a fantastic way to clear ourselves. When we use breathing with intention, we can release all kinds of stuck energy. Most people learn to constrain or limit their breath as children, clamping down on their emotions to avoid showing them. For example, you quickly learn to tightly control your breath to make sure you don't cry on the school playground. As adults we continue this unconscious breathing restriction as an unhealthy but effective way to control our emotions. It's important to break this pattern, so see if you can begin to notice when you constrict your breathing and whether you are trying to clamp down on an emotion.

When you catch yourself restricting your breathing, consciously breathe deeply, bringing air low into your belly, and observe what is happening. What emotion are you holding back? Is it yours or does it belong to someone else? Learning to breathe with intention can help us change our habit of holding back our feelings and holding onto other people's feelings too.

This clearing breath is a powerful and very simple practice that you can do anywhere and at any time.

# CLEARING BREATH

Use this breathing technique to clear your own emotions and also to release any emotions or physical sensations that you might have picked up from other people.

1.  Concentrate on a deep inhale through your nose to your lower belly and exhale strongly through your mouth with a "whoosh" sound. Don't be afraid to make a noise.

2.  Do a little body scan and look for tightness or pain in your body. That is usually a sign that you are holding on to an emotion. Use this breathing pattern and focus your attention on the area of tightness. Breathe deeply through your nose, sending the breath into that area, and then breath out through your mouth with a whoosh.

3.  Is there an emotion or a sensation that you want to release? Does it belong to you or someone else? Imagine that energy leaving your mouth on your exhale. Sometimes the stuck energy and emotion will want to leave through your feet and into the earth via your grounding cord. Or it might want to leave out your hands or even directly from your heart. Allow it to find its natural exit point and let it go.

4.  Repeat the clearing breath until the tension is gone.

I use this clearing breath to release energy when I am having a strong emotion or when I am working on my clients to help them release. If a client is holding on to stuck energy, I use this breathing pattern myself to help release it, and I also ask them to breath.

Now that we have learned how to ground and clear, it's time to learn to replace our lost energy through a process called *filling*.


## Filling

We have already discussed how empaths leak energy from our porous energy fields, which leads to exhaustion—being physically and emotionally drained. We need tools to replace our lost energy every day.

*Filling* is like putting gas back into our energy tank. It's about replenishing ourselves so we can continue to give to others. Empaths are always going to give to others—it's part of our core nature—but most of us never learn how refill ourselves, so we continually give on an empty tank. We burn out but just keep going, feeling like we must earn our right to be here by caretaking others. This leads us to feel resentful and anxious and can have a very negative impact on our health.

By learning to refill our own energy, we can give from a full tank. When we do this, giving to others is a pleasurable experience that fulfills our life purpose and brings us a soul-level joy. As empaths, we are meant to help others, but we must learn to put ourselves first, at the top of the list. This goes against our programming about what "good" people do, but it's vital to work through that myth and make filling yourself a daily habit.

Here are some ways to do it.

## Filling Practices

There are many ways to refill our energy tank; it's a very individual process. But there are some good foundations that we *all* need. Nourishing food is a must. Eat plenty of whole, unprocessed, high-nutrient food, organic as much as possible. When we are burned out, many of us tend to lean too heavily on caffeine, sugar, and junk food, which only stresses our systems further. Establish a habit of nourishing food, and take any necessary supplements for vitamins and minerals that your diet may not provide.

Get plenty of sleep and rest. Make sure you are getting your eight hours a night, and nap when you can and need to. We also need regular daily exercise, and it doesn't have to be a formal gym workout; a brisk walk is good for body and spirit. We tend to drop these basics in stressful circumstances, but that is exactly when we need them the most. If there is an emergency in your life, double down on these basics of caring for your body; make them top of your list, no matter what.

As an empath, you may need to release a false belief that you are a bad person if you give to yourself first. Here is a good exercise for you. Make a list of all the filling things you like to do and put in on your fridge. Next time you feel burned out and want to stick your head in the fridge to eat something, check your list and see if there is something filling that you need to do instead.

Here's an important point, though. Make sure your list includes only activities that are healthy for you. It's good to try and break the habit of using more addictive behaviors to fill ourselves. Empaths often struggle with addictions, and learning healthy ways to replace our lost energy can reduce our dependency on our addictions.

Try to do at least one filling activity every day. You will find you have plenty of time when you prioritize it. I recently cut down my TV watching time and suddenly found myself with hours of extra time every day in which to do some much yummier and more fulfilling activities.

# ACTIVITIES THAT RECHARGE YOUR BATTERY

On top of the basic self-care practices, here are some other powerful filling activities.

- Sunlight is very good for restoring our energy. We need moderate, regular exposure to sunlight to stay healthy. Make sure you take vitamin D in the winter months; a simple blood test will tell you if your levels are low.

- Spiritual practice: This could be a place of worship, a yoga class, a meditation practice, or prayer. Connecting to source helps keep our energy tanks full and our spiritual connection intact.

- Play: This filling pursuit is sadly underrated in our modern world. We all need to play, so get a hobby that appeals to you. Go hiking, play golf, or join a bowling league. Play is one of the most restorative activities that we have. If you revel in solitude, find solo playtime activities; group activities will meet your need to play with others.

- Creative pursuits are also very filling and nurturing. Take up ballroom dancing or painting; learn to play the guitar. Art, crafts, music, and dance are so good for the soul. Observing the arts is healing too, so take in a concert or go to a museum.

- Unstructured time is one of the most powerful ways to fill your energy tank, and it's so rare these days. This means having a chunk of time with nothing to do and nowhere to be. Ah!

Incorporating filling activities in your daily or weekly routine keeps your energy tank and your heart full. When we give from a full place, we have boundless energy for others.

We will touch more on these life-giving filling practices in chapter 7, but for now, let's put it all together with a meditation and breathing practice that you can do every day.

## UP AND DOWN BREATHING PRACTICE

This is a powerful way to ground, clear, and protect yourself any time you need to. I do it when I wake up in the morning and before bed. I also do it in between clients in my office and before and after going into any psychically stressful environment.

1. Sit or stand with your feet on the floor. Have your arms and legs uncrossed, and feel your feet press into the ground.

2. Imagine a beam of light coming into the top of your head. Bright white or rainbow-colored energy works wonderfully. Imagine that this is pure energy straight from the heavens.

3. Take a deep breath into the top of your head and breath this light into your heart and belly.

4. Release that breath on your exhale and connect to your grounding cord. Release anything you are holding onto that is not yours, and also any of your own energy that you don't need right now, down the grounding cord.

5. Repeat this sequence until you feel really clear (it usually takes me about three breaths). Let yourself absorb the pure energy from this source, feeling it fill up any place in you that is tired or in pain or feels stuck. Fill up all the way down to your cells.

6. On your next inhale, pull breath up the grounding cord like you are sucking energy up through a straw.

This is energy from the earth and has a different quality from the spirit energy. Breath this energy all the way up your spine and out the top of your head. Let yourself absorb the earth's energy on each inhale, bringing it to any part of you that needs it.

7. On your exhale, imagine the earth energy fountaining out of the top of your head.

8. Do this until you feel clear and filled (again, it usually takes me about three breaths).

9. Finish by putting the bubble around you. You are grounded, cleared, filled with celestial and earth energy, and protected.

This exercise is one that Remy taught me all those many years ago; he called it the "Tree of Life" meditation. It's interesting to note how different those two sources of energy are. The energy from above is often experienced as white or rainbow colored; the earth energy is warmer, orange or green. As Remy related it, the divine energy has an aspect of divine father and the earth energy an aspect of divine mother—a common human perception talked about in almost all religions and philosophies.

These are pure, unlimited energy sources that we can connect to and pull from any time we need to. It is only when we don't know how to connect to these two sources of energy that we can fall into the bad habit of pulling energy out of other people.

Ideally, we have an even flow of these two streams of energy flowing though us all the time. When we do, we are full all the time and have no need to steal energy from other people. We need a full supply of both of these energy types, and fortunately there is an unlimited supply; they never run out and are constantly available.

We have fully covered how to manage your energy field and ground, clear, fill, and protect yourself. I hope you feel relieved of the burden of holding onto both your own and other people's emotions and energy. You would be all set if you never had to deal with another person, right?

And yet all of us do. Especially we empaths. And often we have to engage with the trickiest of all types, the ones that drain you dry: the energy vampires.

# CHAPTER 4

# Our Dances with Energy Vampires

We have all had times when we have had the energy drained out of us by another person. Maybe it's a friend who talks your ears off for hours about the same problems that they are unwilling to change. Perhaps it's your boss who uses and abuses you, claiming credit for your work while beating down your self-esteem. Or your partner, who can't seem to manage life on their own and drains all your resources—time, attention, and money.

Energy vampires have learned to survive in the world by latching onto other people and draining them. They have an uncanny radar that leads them right to the nearest empath. The energy they take from us can be our life force energy, or it can be our time, attention, and resources like money and credit. It might be energy in the form of the food in your fridge and the gas in your car. An energy vampire will take what is yours as if it's theirs, usually without a thank-you or any idea that they should pay you back for it.

And that is the key. Energy vampires take and take without returning anything, which creates an energy imbalance that will leave you persistently depleted. In healthy relationships, we aim for a general energetic balance in which the energy exchange between people is more or less even over time, and when we have a relationship like that, we don't experience it as draining. When we are in relationship with an energy vampire, there is no reciprocation.

So what exactly is an energy vampire?

Stories of creatures that crawl out of their graves and suck the blood out of living things have been around for as long as human history. Mythical vampires are a powerful and dark part of the human psyche and the collective unconscious. They are an archetypal part of humanity, a piece of us that we need to be aware of and defend ourselves against. Much as the Grimm brothers' fairy tales were an old-fashioned way of warning children about wicked strangers and other dangers, our vampire myths are a way for us to understand and protect ourselves against people who can drain us.

Lately, vampires have risen to prominence in the popular imagination. In the past few decades they have become media darlings, inspiring a host of books, TV shows, and movies. We have been fascinated with vampires, even to the point of revering them. Hollywood vampires are powerful, sexually alluring, hypnotic, and seductive, yet they can't exist without taking the blood, the life force energy of other people. They are parasites who create other vampires by finding a victim and draining their blood and their strength.

And now energy vampires have become part of the conversations among empaths. As we are waking up to our empathic nature, we also becoming aware of our relationships with energy vampires. There is a powerful and unavoidable connection between empaths and energy vampires that can be incredibly healing experience for both, or an epic train wreck.

## What Makes Someone an Energy Vampire?

Here are some common characteristics of energy vampires:

- They take energy from others to sustain themselves in an essentially parasitic relationship.

- The narcissistic type of vampire does this consciously; they are predatory and, in extreme cases, can be very dangerous.

- The victim type of vampire drags down everyone around them with their lack of personal empowerment.

- The situational energy vampire is usually unconsciously responding to a difficult but temporary situation. We are all susceptible to becoming one of these.

- Even an empath can become an energy vampire if they let themself get too drained.

Most of us haven't learned how to properly manage our energy, so we steal energy from each other. Energy vampirism is a process that anyone can fall into and sometimes empaths are the worst offenders.

The world is full of natural energy-givers and natural energy-takers. In the grand scheme of the universe, there is a rightness to this pattern. Eileen McKusick, founder of Biofield Tuning and author of the book *Tuning the Human Biofield: Healing with Vibrational Sound Therapy,*[4] describes people as either natural electron donors or electron stealers. Some people are more naturally inclined to be giving; we call these people empaths, sensitives, and healers. Some other people are takers; we call these people narcissists and, at their worst, energy vampires.

In an ideal world, energy would balance out between people over time, with all of us giving and receiving from each other equally. McKusick says that a natural flow of energy creates an electric current between people when they interact, and this natural rhythm creates a healthy energetic flow between people.

I see these types as two sides of a natural polarity, often pulled into relationships and interactions. We exist with each other as opposite ends of a spectrum, and as we learn to dance with each other we can learn much that is very good for us. Yet if we are to be empowered in these relationships, we must learn to tell whether we are getting drained.

# How to Tell if You Are Getting Drained

When an energy vampire is draining you, you can be sure that you will feel something. It's very good to know the symptoms so you can recognize when this is happening. There have been times when I knew an energy vampire was around because I had the feeling first. Once I started to recognize the feeling, I would look around and find the vampire. If you are getting drained, you are likely to feel some of the following symptoms.

## Exhaustion and Depletion

I know that if I need a nap after talking to someone, the person is an energy vampire who has been draining my energy. I remember, as a teenager, literally lying down on the couch at my friend's house and falling asleep. It was very rude of me, I am sure!

My friend's mother was undergoing treatment for lung cancer, but she refused to stop smoking. She was a powerfully needy victim vampire, sucking the life out of my poor friend, who was an empath herself and had been drained to the point of going vampire herself. The energy in the house was about as bad as it gets. After an hour of trying to be supportive to my friend, I just lay down and conked out. I was simply unable to keep my eyes open any longer.

If you notice that you always feel exhausted after an interaction with someone, there is a good chance that person is pulling on your energy and might be an energy vampire.

## A Tugging or Pulling Sensation at the Solar Plexus

Watch your own body language. If you find that you are crossing your arms over your solar plexus to cover it up, you might be getting drained. Energy vampires love to hook us right in this energy center, which manages our personal power. The energy vampire will energetically tug on that place in an attempt to dominate us.

My friend Matt told me a story about meeting a famous politician:

*The man was powerful and very charismatic. As he shook my hand, he pulled me into his solar plexus so that my hand was literally touching that part of him. He held my gaze and pulled me almost off my feet so that I stumbled toward him. He also put his hand over mine with his on top, literally taking the upper hand and leaving me off balance.*

Matt said he felt sort of scooped out at his solar plexus after that:

*His eyes were like a basilisk's glare, hard and cold. All his body language was about power over me and domination and grabbing at my energy.*

## An Occipital Headache

The occiput is at the back of the head, right above where your neck joins your skull. Many people report a dull throbbing headache at this point after an encounter with an energy vampire. We have a strongly psychic energy center back there that can feel under attack when an energy vampire is playing head games with us. This energy center, called the *zeal point* or the *awakening point* in energy healing, is always collecting information from our other energy centers to bring us deeply psychic aha! moments. When someone is playing mind games or shape shifting, and the energy we feel from them doesn't match their spoken energy, we can get an occipital headache. Their words might be seductive and appealing, while the energy we are feeling from them feels dangerous. This disconnect blows a circuit back there, and the pain comes when we attempt to shut down the connection with the vampire.

## Nightmares

Bad dreams, especially recurring ones, can be a sign that someone is draining you. When an energy vampire connects to us psychically, we will feel an energy drain through a strong psychic connection that is most powerful at night and in our dreams. Many energy vampires, especially the predatory ones, are skilled at a psychic connection that is meant to drain you while you are sleeping. It's easy to do then, since when we are sleeping we are unguarded and vulnerable.

## A Feeling of Dread or Resentment

This is a sure sign that someone is draining you. We all have to deal with unpleasant people, but if you regularly have a serious feeling of dread, chances are good that they are draining you and maybe even psychically attacking you. Predatory vampires often inspire dread in people; the back of your brain knows that you are the prey and they are the predator.

Resentment comes when we are dealing with a victim vampire; it's a normal reaction to an imbalance in our give-and-take with a person. We feel resentful when we consistently give more than we receive and it's an important red flag to notice. In chapter 5 we will do a deep dive into how to deal with this dynamic in an empowering way.

## The Dance Between the Empath and the Energy Vampire

Let's take a look at the dance between Shailene and Miles, whose journey together, although challenging at times, also demonstrates the beautiful healing that is possible between an empath and a person with energy vampire tendencies.

Shailene is an empath and a natural-born healer. While working as a nurse in a veteran's hospital, she met Miles, who was there for treatment for PTSD. Miles had served in Iraq and Afghanistan and experienced his fair share of combat as a weapons specialist. He was charming and handsome and appealed to the healer in Shailene.

"I fell in love at first sight and just knew I could help him," she said. "All he needed was a little love."

This is a belief that many empaths share. We know that we are healers and that our love can heal people if they will simply allow themselves to be loved. Although that can be true, those people need to be committed to their own healing or it becomes another unhealthy, codependent relationship.

After they moved in together, Miles's behavior changed. He fell into a deep depression and had fits of rage. He stopped working and started drinking and smoking marijuana. Shailene would come home from work and find the house trashed and Miles passed out on the couch. When Shailene cried about the state of their life and relationship, Miles would listen and agree but then bounce right back to his old disruptive patterns. Shailene started suffering from a decline in her health and energy levels too. She was exhausted, and no matter how much she slept, she never felt rested. She lost a lot of weight and looked like she had aged during this time too. At one point during this period, I saw them together, and while she looked frail, shaky and thin, he was glowing with robust energy, despite his unhealthy lifestyle.

Shailene told me, "I feel like he is sucking the life out of me. He says he loves me, but I feel like I am losing ground in my life." She worked hard to find her boundary and did a lot work with her team of healers to learn how to love herself enough to stand up for herself in the relationship. One day, she found out that Miles had pawned the contents of her jewelry box, including some treasured family heirlooms, and that was her breaking point. She had had enough. She told Miles that although she loved him, she needed him to move out.

"He could see in my eyes that I meant it. And I did. I was one hundred percent ready to walk away out of self-respect," said Shailene.

Miles got the message and pulled himself together. He joined an AA group that focused on supporting veterans, and within a few weeks he was clean and sober. This gave him enough energy to get a construction job and bring in money. With sobriety and his self-respect back, he improved steadily over time, getting therapy, working with a VA support group, and learning Reiki.

It was a long, bumpy journey for the both of them. Shailene continued to hold her boundary and communicate what she needed every day. She discovered that holding onto herself and not getting lost in his needs was a daily practice that continued to challenge her every day. This was a muscle that she needed to flex in all her relationships, which improved as a result of the work she was doing.

Miles had his work to do too. He was able to maintain his sobriety and over time worked his way up through the ranks to a foreman job. He does Reiki with other veterans, sponsors people in AA, and recently proposed to Shailene.

This story could have gone another way, but it is a heartwarming example of what can be possible when an empath and an energy vampire come together. It's important to understand that each of them had to do their part to get to their happy ending, and if either of them hadn't, it would have ended in disaster and heartbreak.

Shailene's part of the dance was to learn how to set a boundary and stick with it, no matter what. That required that she feel so much self-worth that she could say no to Miles's behavior even though she loved him. She read books on codependency, went to Al-Anon meetings, and worked on strengthening her energetic boundary. She had to take many steps along the empath–energy vampire continuum to actually become more "selfish," and she has continued to work this edge every day.

In the middle of this continuum is a point that psychologists call *healthy narcissism*, which means that we have good self-esteem and value ourselves enough that we refuse to sacrifice ourself for someone else. This breaks the pattern of codependency, which is where empaths often find themselves until they do this work.

Miles also had his choices to make. He later told me that it was love that saved him. "Shailene was the best thing that ever happened to me. There was a broken part of me that felt like I didn't deserve that love, and I was so depressed that all I could do was take from her. I had nothing left of myself to give to her."

It took a lot of external support for Miles to heal, and it required a daily commitment to stay with his sobriety and do the inner work that he needed to heal. He said that a turning point was when his therapist asked him to consider how Shailene must have felt when he sold her jewelry.

"I was so wrapped up in my own pain, I never thought of how anyone else felt. Ever. I know it sounds horrible, but up until that moment, I never in my whole life considered how other people felt or that my words and actions could hurt someone."

Miles felt empathy for the first time, and it completely changed his life. He moved along the spectrum away from narcissism and toward empathy, and this motivated him to work with other veterans. "I committed to working with the veterans to keep myself feeling empathy for other people. It was a muscle that I needed to use a lot at first, since I would start to go back to my old ways if I didn't."

This is what is possible in the dance between the empath and the energy vampire, and why there is a chance for healing when these opposite poles meet each other. Every time an empath encounters an energy vampire, there is an opportunity for healing and for strengthening both parties.

For the energy vampires, every encounter with an empath gives them an opportunity for the healing that empaths offer. And the energy vampire can learn to open their heart in compassion and accept the powerful spiritual gift of empathy.

Again, this story had a happy ending because both Shailene and Miles were committed to doing the necessary inner work. It doesn't always work out well, and sometimes our encounters with energy vampires can be dangerous if we are not prepared. Let's take a look at the four different types of energy vampire and how to recognize them.

## The Predatory Energy Vampire

When we think of energy vampires, this is the image that most springs to mind: the heartless con artist who callously drains their victims before throwing them away. Predatory energy vampires fall into this category. Fortunately, they are relatively rare, but there is a chance that you will run into one at some point.

If you know anything about the extreme narcissistic or psychopathic personality type, you are well on your way to understanding the predatory energy vampire. This type of person feels empty inside and lacks the ability to feel empathy for others. At their worst, they are parasitic and predatory, seeing other people as objects whose sole function is to fill their needs. Much like the Hollywood version of a vampire, they see people as energetic food to be consumed, useful only as an energy supply. Thus they can't see the value of compassion or empathy; rather, they see these as weaknesses they can exploit without remorse.

This type of behavior is so alien to an empath that we are often blindsided by a predatory energy vampire's behavior. We never see it coming, since we can't even think that way. Empaths are always putting ourselves in someone else's shoes, always thinking about how other people will feel about what we say and do; it's as natural to us as breathing. The predatory vampire knows this and uses it to their advantage.

They will search for a likely victim that they feel that they can easily control and manipulate, with the conscious goal of taking that person for all they are worth. There is an unapologetic entitlement in this. They feel they deserve to be served by others and will often say that the world "owes" them something—or everything. They also show a profound level of loathing for anyone who is stupid enough to fall for their tricks. They are consummate con artists, looking for a mark by using their uncanny ability to sniff out who might be vulnerable to their attentions. Once they sense our weak spots, they proceed to shapeshift into being exactly what we need and want them to be.

Like the classic vampires portrayed by Hollywood, many predatory energy vampires are highly attractive, charming, and alluring, at least on the surface. Like any good con artist, they can act the part, shapeshifting so perfectly that they can sneak past our guard, fooling even the highly sensitive empaths, who usually deeply understand other people.

They can charm the pants off us, shower us with love and affection, and appear to be perfectly attuned to our every need. This process is called *love bombing*, and to most empaths this stage of the relationship feels like a dream come true. Just as a fisherman sets the hook with a big, juicy worm, the predatory energy vampire feeds you what you want most in the world until you are hooked. Then suddenly the stakes change and you are asked to give, give, and give some more.

Essentially parasitic, a predatory energy vampire will siphon energy in all its forms from you. In her book *Dodging Energy Vampires: An Empath's Guide to Evading Relationships that Drain You and Restoring Your Health And Power,*[5] Dr. Christiane Northrup says that this type of energy vampire is part of the Cluster B personality disorders—antisocial, narcissistic, and borderline personality disorders—according to the *Diagnostic and Statistical Manual of Mental Disorders, 5th edition (DSM-5),*[6] the reference book that psychiatrists use to classify mental health conditions.

Unfortunately, we live in a world that appears to admire the narcissists among us. These public personalities—be they performers, athletes, politicians, or reality stars—pose for their selfies and live lives bent on instant gratification, at the expense of anyone who might get in their way. Their fans and followers on social media desire to be like them, and they let them get away with all kinds of bad behavior.

Recently, I worked with a young man who fell in love and gave his narcissistic energy vampire girlfriend everything he had. Sean told me, "When I first met Natalie, it appeared as if she was so confident, in control of her life, and she was so sexy. She seduced me into a relationship that I wasn't looking for."

Sean explained that Natalie used her powerful sex appeal to catch his interest. "She is very beautiful, but once she had me hooked, I started to see the cracks in her image. She was basically needy, insecure, and full of anxiety. She needed money, so I gave her everything I had and maxed out my credit cards. She always wanted me to buy her things, and soon I was paying her rent. She quit her job and started partying a lot. If I complained, she would pout, cry, or throw a tantrum."

Natalie would withhold love, sex, and attention to punish Sean if he didn't give her what she wanted.

He said, "Just when I would be on the brink of breaking up with her, she would pour on the charm and affection and turn the sex on again, and I would relent."

Sean told me that it wasn't until his friends staged an intervention for him that he started to see Natalie for who she really was: an unrepentant predatory energy vampire. "She wasn't interested in fixing herself or changing," he said. "She never wanted to work on our relationship, and she pointed out that if I was unhappy, I could leave, and that there were plenty of other guys who would jump at the chance of dating her, which was true. She would tell me what she thought I wanted to hear and then go back to her old ways."

Soon after the intervention, Sean found out that Natalie had another man on the side who was also giving her money and buying her things. Sean ended it, and Natalie moved on, totally unremorseful. Her parting words to Sean were that she was on her way up, that he was a steppingstone to a better place for her, and it was his fault he couldn't take her to the next level of money and status that she was looking for.

Sean was left with a mountain of debt, a hit to his self-esteem, and a broken heart. Fortunately, he started therapy and could begin to see the relationship as a powerful learning experience.

"I started to see that I didn't need to take it personally; it's just the way she is. In the end, I couldn't even blame her," he said. "A shark is a shark, and if you get in the water with them, they might bite you, since that is what sharks do."

Sean learned an important, albeit painful lesson about choosing his partners. Of course, it's not just lovers who are predatory energy vampires. They come in all kinds of roles—best friend, boss, family member. Whatever their relationship to you is, it's important to be able to spot one, hopefully before they hook you.

## Spotting a Predatory Energy Vampire

This narcissist will hoodwink you easily, so an empath must have their wits about them in order to spot one. Here are some common characteristics.

- They are shapeshifters, capable of morphing into whatever you need and want them to be. They adopt your hobbies, cultivate your friends, and fulfill whatever fantasy desire you reveal to them.

- During the love bombing or honeymoon stage, they will smother you with love and attention, setting the hook expertly.

- They use their frighteningly accurate psychic ability to feel where your weaknesses are and what your desires are; then they exploit the weaknesses and fulfill the desires.

- Once the hook is set, they will begin to systematically drain you. They suddenly need money, time, and attention and always have a sob story about why nothing is ever their fault.

- They usually have a jealous, possessive side and will try to isolate you from your friends and family.

- If you fight against this hook, they become manipulative and even abusive. They seem like two people, one good and one evil. You get the good side when you comply with their wishes and the evil side when you don't. They are masters of the carrot and the stick.

- They are fundamentally empty and have no way to fill themselves without draining you. At any attempt to break free, they will level up the charm, and if that doesn't work, they'll level up the abuse.

- They are unrepentant and can't or won't change; they see themselves as perfect and you as the problem. Cut them loose as soon as you can.

If you have encountered one of these predatory energy vampires, chances are good that they really took a bite out of you. It took me years of dedicated work to recover from a relationship with one of these types. You can and should do all the healing work that you need to in order to recover.

## Getting Out and Recovering

When you are dealing with a predatory energy vampire, the best thing to do is cut your losses and get away as soon as you can, since there is no chance of redeeming them. The other kinds of energy vampires can learn empathy if they choose to, but this predatory kind not only can't, but simply don't want to. In their eyes, you are the problem, and if you establish a boundary and start saying no to their manipulations, they will leave and move on to someone more accommodating, with no remorse, and blaming you all the way.

It is difficult for an empath to understand the predatory energy vampire, since we truly believe that we can and should heal people with our loving care and attention. However, in this case it's like opening up a vein and draining your blood out onto sand. No amount of your time, energy, and money will be enough to fill what is basically an emptiness inside another person.

If you feel that you have become entangled with a predatory energy vampire, get as much support as you can and find a way to disentangle yourself as soon as you can. Like the Hollywood vampires, these folks can have a hypnotic effect on an empath, so it might take help to get out of it. Marshal your resources and plan an escape if you need to.

Fortunately for empaths, there is a worldwide narcissistic abuse recovery movement that offers many great resources for helping people recover, all of which apply to people who have been damaged by a relationship with a predatory energy vampire. There are books, recovery groups, workshops, online forums, and YouTube videos, as well as many therapists who specialize in helping people recover from these toxic relationships.

I recommend these books: *The Human Magnet Syndrome: The Codependent Narcissist Trap*, by Ross Rosenburg,[7] and *Narcissist Abuse Recovery: A Guide to Finding Clarity and Reclaiming Your Joy After Leaving a Toxic Relationship* by Emma Chan.[8] It helps to know that you are not alone and help is available.

I hope that by now you fully understand what a predatory energy vampire looks like and how to get out of those relationships. And although the predatory energy vampire is what comes to mind when we think of an energy vampire, thankfully it's the rarest kind. You are much more likely to encounter the next type of energy vampire: the needy victim kind. Although they are less blatantly destructive than the predatory energy vampire, they can take a toll on us, especially over the long haul.

## The Needy Victim Energy Vampire

This type of energy vampire can really sneak up on you. They don't have the bone-chilling, blood-sucking, con artist qualities of the predatory energy vamps; in fact, they are often unassuming and can even appear fragile and needy. These vamps have learned that by playing the victim, they can get a massive supply of energy and attention from other people. They have learned to use their victim status as a kind of currency.

Some victim energy vampires are very purposely manipulative; others are very unconscious about their behaviors and the ways that they impact other people. To be clear, many people have been legitimately victimized through no fault of their own, and I am not blaming the victim here. However, we all have choices we can make about how we are going to handle it. Carolyn Myss says that trauma can either cripple you or initiate you, and that we have that choice. It's our responsibility to clean up any trauma that we have endured and not allow that to be a rationalization for becoming an energy vampire.

In her book *Why People Don't Heal and How They Can,*[9] Carolyn Myss talks about *woundology,* her term for when people use their victim status as a way to gain power over other people. People who take the empowerment path allow whatever happened to them to become a pathway to personal and spiritual growth. They get healings, go to therapy, join support groups, start foundations, or help other people who are traveling along the same path.

The victim energy vampire, in contrast, learns that they can use their victim status as a kind of power over others, a way to latch on and suck energy from everyone else. They often come across as helpless, needy, and requiring a lot of assistance due to their issues. If they don't get what they need and want, however, they quickly use a series of manipulations to increase pressure on you until you give in. Guilt is their weapon of choice, and they can wield that weapon like a samurai sword master.

## Identifying a Victim Energy Vampire

I recently overheard this conversation at a restaurant. It was Mother's Day, and at the table next to me was a small, frail elderly woman and her three extra-large, extra-sweet sons. She continually needed them to adjust things, fetch and carry for her, and fix what was wrong with her meal. She kept up a constant stream of complaints, from the weather to the food, her health, the state of the world, and especially her good-for-nothing daughters-in-law (who mercifully were not in attendance).

It went something like this: "Don't you know how hard it was to carry you in my womb for nine months, and then you almost killed me on the way out? How I have suffered for you! And I brought you into this world and gave you your life! The least you can do is get me a fresh iced tea. Not too much ice…"

The three men rolled their eyes, but only behind her back. To her face, they snapped to at her every command, and she was clearly enjoying every minute of it. "Why do we put up with this?" one of them asked the other two.

"Because it's family and she is our mother. And it's the only fun she gets."

Yikes! Such a great example of a victim energy vampire at work.

The needy victim energy vampire may not consciously know this is what they are, but they can drain you dry if you are not careful. If you are in a relationship with a victim energy vampire, I guarantee it's a codependent relationship, and there is a lot you can do to empower both yourself and the vampire. We will go fully into this dynamic and how to skillfully navigate it in chapter 5, as we learn to set a healthy boundary. For now, let's look at how to spot one of these before they get their needy hooks into you.

## Common Characteristics of the Victim Energy Vampire

- A victim vampire has something "wrong" with them—an illness, an addiction, or a lifestyle problem that is genuinely hard to manage—which gives them power and leverage over their caretakers.

- They take energy from you by grabbing your attention and complaining. They love a good complaint!

- They are not interested in getting better or moving toward a healthier life, so they don't take even the most obvious action to better their situation. They often ask for advice and help but never take it.

- Usually they make decisions that add to their drama and trauma, which is fresh fuel for the fire. They have a knack of making the worst possible decisions.

- They use guilt to manipulate and control.

- They have a "poor me" attitude that they think gives them license to behave badly.

- They use emotional manipulation to get what they want, whining and pouting or throwing a temper tantrum in turns, until you finally give in.

Once you have spotted a victim vampire, you will need to end your codependent relationship with them.

Here is a great example of a needy victim energy vampire from my friend and colleague Jess.

*I started my healing practice fourteen years ago, and I was very excited about being of service to people but totally unaware of what an energy vampire is, especially the needy kind. I had a new client I will call Cara. She had a lot of issues and dwelled a lot on the past, but she came every week for sessions, so I thought that she was committed to her growth and eager to do the work. She often tried to control the session and would email in between with very long messages of her feelings and her problems, and there was an element of blame in her communications. She would insinuate that if I was a good healer I should give more and that it was my fault that she still had problems and didn't feel well.*

*I kept trying to be of assistance but never seemed to be effective in helping her. She never moved beyond her pain and didn't seem to want any guidance on how to do so. I found myself starting to think of her often. I would think of ways of helping her, or I would read a book and think, Wow, this could help Cara. I started to realize it wasn't healthy to think of her like this, so I would try to redirect my thoughts, but a short time later my thoughts would creep back to her.*

*One night I had a powerful dream. In the dream I was in my car driving to her house. As I was driving to her house, my car battery was dying. The lights were dimming as if my alternator wasn't working. Eventually the car broke down. As I sat in my car in the dream, I decided to turn the car around. It started and I was able to turn around and head back to my home. The closer I got to home, the more power came back to my car. Once I got home, I looked out the front window and saw that the house was surrounded by vampires. I was terrified and thought to myself They can only get in if I invite them in!*

*Then I woke up. As I came to full wakefulness, I realized that I was dealing with a psychic vampire and needed to set a boundary. I contacted Cara that day and told her I could no longer see her; that I felt the sessions weren't assisting her and she would be better off finding a licensed therapist. She wasn't happy, but I never dreamed of her again, nor did my thoughts stray to her ever again.*

For those of us not wired that way, it's hard to comprehend why someone would actually enjoy being a victim. They have no incentive to heal because their victim status allows them to get what they need from all of the accommodating people around them. They will easily suck in a compassionate empath, since we can really feel their pain. Again, I am not diminishing the fact that we all go through difficult things, but we have a choice to either wallow in them and milk them for all they're worth, or do our inner work and let those challenging events help us find our power.

Sometimes the victim energy vampires do their energy sucking in a very unconscious way. Unlike the predatory energy vampires, who are highly conscious of what they are doing, the victim vampires don't usually wake up in the morning thinking *How can I suck the life out of Lisa today?* They are just hustling and trying to get by the best that they can and have learned a habit of taking from others. Some of them are horrified to find out that they are energy vampires, although they don't realize that they have now become victimizers, and they are not always ready to change their ways. I have also met some victim energy vamps who know full well what they are doing and are unwilling to change and give up their energy-draining ways.

Chapter 5 is all about learning to set healthy boundaries for yourself and thereby liberating yourself from the needy victim energy vamps. Fortunately, if you take the necessary step of resetting the boundary, a victim energy vampire will usually adjust.

Sometimes the victim energy vampire will choose to empower themself and let go of their victim status. That is something worth celebrating. If you recognized yourself in that description, I urge you to take a deep look at the toll your victim addiction has taken on other people and how it might have stunted your own growth and development. Empaths can all too easily feel victimized by all of our encounters with energy vampires and the rigors of living in a tough world. If you feel ready to change and drop your identification with your victim status, chapter 7 is for you; it's all about how to recover if you have fallen into being a vampire yourself.

Now that we know how to spot a victim energy vampire and what to do to heal the victim aspects of ourselves, let's take a look at the next type of energy vampire.

## The Situational Energy Vampire

By now you might be realizing that some energy vampires are not so much a particular kind of person but the result of a process that can happen to the best of us, if we let our energy be drained too low. Life circumstances can knock down normally strong people to the point of becoming energy vampires.

I call the person who reaches this point a *situational* energy vampire, since the condition is usually temporary, stemming from the less-than-ideal situation that they may be in. It might be a bad breakup, the loss of a loved one, losing a job, or a dealing with a debilitating health condition. We all may fall on hard times, and in that situation we are not at our best. Under pressing circumstances we can become very needy and energy-depleted, and if we don't know how to properly manage our energy, we become an energy vampire too, draining the people who are trying to support us.

Swamped by a trauma and tragedy, anyone can temporarily become a situational energy vampire. Life can challenge us to our very core, leaving us feeling desperate, ill, despondent, and hopeless. We might also feel like a victim and latch onto the people around us to save ourselves from drowning. It might be something like this:

- A big change in your life's circumstances, like the loss of a job or a loved one

- A challenging health condition or illness

- A natural disaster like a fire, flood, storm damage, or a pandemic

- Economic disaster that creates a struggle for survival

- A change in mental health status, like chronic anxiety or severe depression

Anything that throws us into survival mode can make us an unwitting and unwilling energy vampire.

Kavita is a very strong woman and runs her own company as high-level executive recruiter. She is also the matriarch of her family and finds a way to support everyone she knows with her big heart, creative problem solving, and generous nature. And yet everything crashed down around her when she got a diagnosis of breast cancer at age forty-nine. This required surgery and a heavy round of chemotherapy that left her feeling very weak and depleted. During this time, Kavita's mother had a catastrophic stroke, and one of her adult children entered a substance abuse recovery program. This was more than she could handle in her weakened state, and she began to suffer from panic attacks.

"I can't stop crying," she told me in a healing session. "I am usually the strong one, and I have no strength now. I don't want to pull on my children for help, since everyone is in bad shape, but I feel like I am going down. I hate the feeling of not being able to help or fix things, but I am barely holding on myself."

Kavita began pay attention to how she was handling this stress when she noticed that her friends started avoiding her and not taking her calls. "I realized that I had been calling them at all hours, crying and complaining and sometimes being hysterical. As hard as this is, I realized that I have to fix this myself. Sometimes we just have to go through hard things."

Kavita and I worked together while she was at this low point, and she was able to get out of her situational energy vampire mode by marshaling her resources. She connected with the visiting nurses for more help for herself and to help her mother get into a hospice. She also started working regularly with me and a therapist to help her manage all her feelings in a more productive way. And eventually her life stabilized. Her mother passed away peacefully in hospice care around the same time that Kavita completed her cancer treatment and got a clean bill of health. Shortly after that, her son finished his rehab, and he has remained sober. Kavita learned a powerful lesson about giving herself what she needed so that she could stay out of energy vampire mode.

Our goal with our loved ones is to have a fifty-fifty relationship over a period of time. If we have a more or less even flow of energy over the long term, then our network of people will have extra time for us when we are brought down by difficult circumstances. It's a bit like managing a bank account with someone. If you take too much credit out without putting it back in, you are running into an energetic debt with the other person. But as long as things even out over time, more or less, you will have energetic equality in your relationships. Kavita made a point of giving back to her friends after all they had done for her during her time of hardship, and by doing so, she rebalanced the energy between them.

There is much you can do to support yourself through the inevitable tough times. These are also good measures to use if you know someone else who is experiencing a crisis that has turned them into a situational energy vampire:

- Take a good look at the resources available; there is often help to be had all around us. Get practical support from the visiting nurses or social service agencies.

- Find a way to receive emotional support from as many sources as you can. Therapy, body work, journaling, and meditating can really help.

- Stick to your self-care regimen. Get enough sleep, eat well, and exercise regularly. We tend to drop these things under pressure right when we need them the most.

- If you are really stuck, ask your supporters to help you plan; there are many great online resources like Caringbridge.com for meal trains and comfort measures.

When we go down hard in a crisis, we can forget that there is help available all around, if we will just ask for it. It can make all the difference in keeping us from becoming a situational energy vampire. If you are dealing with someone else in this situation who is draining you, don't be afraid to set a boundary. We will learn how to do just that with grace and ease in the next chapter.

# CHAPTER 5

# Saying No and Defending Our Psychic Space

By now, you have realized how important it is to have boundaries. Yet the more sensitive you are, the harder it is to create and maintain these. In this chapter you will learn, step by step when to create a boundary and how to do it effectively.

When we have a strong boundary, energy vampires tend to wander off in search of easier prey. The needy victim or predatory energy vampires seem to have an effective detector for personal boundaries; they can sniff out where your boundary is and how strong it is in about thirty seconds.

Let's begin by learning what I mean by a personal boundary.

## Understanding Boundaries

What is a boundary? Non-empathic people usually have no problem answering that question. They intrinsically know that a boundary is an inherent separation between people that they feel in a few different ways.

Psychologists define a boundary as the limits of our personal space, a set of rules and guidelines that help us create reasonable, safe, and appropriate ways for people to connect with us socially, physically, mentally, emotionally, and sexually. This means that we get to be in charge of who touches us, who is in our space, what we think, how we feel, and how we choose to express ourselves sexually. Boundaries are the rules we use to figure out how to let people interact with us and what to do when someone oversteps those boundaries.

There are a few different types of boundaries. Some people have rigid boundaries; others have spongy boundaries or even no boundaries at all. We have been talking about the spongy boundaries of empaths and the lack of boundaries of energy vampires. People with rigid boundaries have trouble letting people approach them at all.

Our boundaries, or lack thereof, are learned and modeled from our family of origin. You can look at your family and see if you can figure out what kind of boundaries you have and how you got them. The more dysfunctional your family, the worse the boundaries are going to be.

An effective boundary has these characteristics:

- It arises out of an inner sense of selfhood, from the solar plexus energy center, creating a knowing that we are separate from others.

- This selfhood is contained in an energy field within a solid container, like a cell with a cell membrane.

- This selfhood is experienced as *I am inside my container and you are not in here with me. This is me, and that is the world, which is not me.*

- From this sense of sovereignty of the self comes a strong feeling of worthiness that gives us permission to say no.

- This means that our self and our needs are just as important as or even more important than those of others.

- A boundary enables us to say yes to what we want and no to what we don't want, without giving up ourself for someone else's needs.

In sum, having a strong boundary means having a strong energy field with a solid barrier layer and also knowing when and how to say yes and no, all of which arises out of having a healthy sense of self.

Our boundaries can be physical, emotional, mental, spiritual, and even digital.

Physical boundaries allow you to decide who can touch you—and when. You are in charge of who can touch you casually, affectionately, and sexually. Physical boundaries also include reproductive and health boundaries, meaning that you can decide your reproductive and health care options. And physical boundaries determine who gets to occupy your physical space and who shares your room or your bed; it includes your material objects, too.

Sexual boundaries are incredibly important and so easily and frequently violated. Sadly, we live in a world where people's sexual boundaries are overrun all the time and vulnerable people are brainwashed into thinking that they don't have a right to say no or that it's okay to ignore someone's no. When we have a strong sexual boundary, we say yes or no about who we want to engage with sexually and how far down that road we want to go. Sexual boundaries also allow us to choose a gender expression and our unique preferences for our partners. Healthy sexual boundaries also allow us to claim a sexual identity if we so choose, or leave it fluid if we don't. Good sexual boundaries mean that you also allow other people to have those same freedoms.

Emotional boundaries mean that we are responsible only for our own emotions and not for other people's emotions. This is an easy one for empaths to blur, especially when someone says something like "You made me so angry!" In a world with good emotional boundaries, everyone owns and takes responsibility for their own emotions. Your emotions are yours to deal with, and you don't have to caretake other people's feelings.

Having healthy mental boundaries means that you are able to think freely and decide for yourself and express your own politics, opinions, philosophies, and beliefs. We are allowed to think for ourselves, with no one else forcing us to adopt their opinions. Having spiritual boundaries is similar; you are allowed to choose your own religious and faith traditions for yourself. You can choose to believe in a god(s) or not, and you are free to allow your beliefs to evolve and change as you grow.

In our modern world, we must also include digital boundaries in the mix. You have the right to access information freely and also deny people access to your digital life. Your passwords on your phone, your text conversations and emails should be yours and yours alone, and no one has the right to demand that you share them. That also means that you must honor that boundary in other people too, since boundaries always go both ways.

We can and should draw boundaries around all our resources—our time, our money, our attention. Having good boundaries means that you manage your right to say yes and no in all these areas, and for most of us it's an ongoing and ever-evolving front line. You also allow other people to have their boundaries. We must learn to say no when we need to and also respect other people's no.

Let's look at an example of someone working hard on these levels.

Tammy's biggest challenge in setting boundaries came at her workplace. She is the executive assistant to three different executives at a big bank in Boston. I met Tammy at one of my energy management workshops, which she was attending because she knew she needed to work on setting boundaries with her bosses.

She explained, "I was told when I was hired that my three bosses were demanding but fair, but they had not been able to keep an assistant for very long. Everyone else who had held the position before ended up quitting after a few months. But I really needed the job, so I took it, determined to make it work for all of us."

Tammy had a brief honeymoon period with her bosses in which they were respectful and appreciative of her, but soon came the demands to do extra. "Within a month, they were piling more and more on my plate. I was working over sixty hours a week and doing the job of two people. I was exhausted and cranky, and my kids and husband were starting to suffer. And I never even got a thank-you or any appreciation. In fact, the more I did, the more they disrespected me. One of them would barge into my office without knocking and take files off my desk. I even caught one of them looking through my phone—searching, he claimed, for a lost email or text."

Tammy was learning one of the biggest rules about boundaries. We train people how to treat us; by agreeing to their expectations, we reinforce the idea that we are slaves to their whims. The fear of losing her well-paying job kept Tammy in this trap until the situation escalated to the point that she knew she had to set a boundary.

"I had to work weekends at home to catch up with everything, and all of a sudden they expected me to be on call twenty-four hours a day. I got a panicked call at two a.m. from one of them, on a Saturday night. He screamed at me for being unavailable to do something he needed right then, and that was when I had had enough."

Tammy practiced the grounding, clearing, and protecting exercises that we learned in chapter 3, and she uncovered some beliefs from her childhood that she was still holding on to: that powerful men who are in charge should not be challenged.

Tammy talked to her human resources department, who helped her set up a meeting with her bosses. In this meeting she confronted them with their bad behavior and lack of respect and appreciation and their poor boundaries. She told them that she would give her notice if their behavior did not change. The group came up with reasonable work hours for Tammy and agreed to hire an assistant for her to help with the workload.

"At first, I really had to stick to my guns; when one of them would cross the boundary, I would remind them of our agreement and say no to the request. It took a lot of hard work, every day, to hold the line with them, I could tell they were pushing me to see if I really meant it. I would say no, firmly and politely, to their requests when I needed to, or push the time back on things, letting them know that they could not contact me on the weekends or past six p.m. in the evenings."

Tammy found that being consistent and nonreactive was the key. Eventually, they learned where Tammy's new boundary was, and she noticed that they were more grateful and respectful toward her.

"The really tough one even started saying 'thank you' on a regular basis and admitted that he had been out of line and offered an apology. No one barged into my office anymore; they knocked politely, and they stopped yelling at me too."

Tammy had successfully learned a few very important lessons on how to set boundaries:

- We train people how to treat us, and if we don't like it, we can change it.

- It takes consistency and nonreactivity to retrain people.

- When we have a strong boundary, people respect us.

Tammy's story is great example of how learning to set boundaries in one area flows through all aspects of our lives, and we never stop being challenged to learn new ways to do this.

## Good Boundaries Are Flexible

One of the most important lessons that I have learned is to be forgiving of myself when I slip a boundary. Boundaries are not rigid, and often we have to feel our way through our boundaries, moment by moment. I often don't know that I have stepped over my own boundary until after the fact. I might say yes to something and then realize it is not feeling right anymore. In that case, we can and should be able to renegotiate our boundary.

# BOUNDARY SETTING BASICS

These basic points will help you build up the internal "muscles" you need for boundary setting.

- When we feel anger or resentment, it's a good indicator that we need to set a boundary.

- It is up to you to communicate your boundaries. No one can do this for you, and no one can read your mind about where your boundaries are. Learn to state these clearly and constantly.

- An effective boundary needs to be flexible, not rigid—except when it comes to your safety.

- Say no and set your conditions using simple language. Don't explain, justify, or apologize.

- Strive for a calm and courteous demeanor. Find a time when you are not triggered, and practice what you need to say beforehand.

- Let the other person deal with their own feelings about your boundary. Chances are good they will have a reaction; that is not yours to fix or caretake.

- Expect them to test the boundary to see if you really mean it. Decide beforehand what the consequence will be, and let them know in your initial conversation.

- Be prepared to execute the consequence, which might mean you need to leave the relationship or job.

If you need it, seek help and support in holding onto your boundary.

Recently, I was asked to be a committee member for an organization that I really believe in. When I was asked, I said yes, but as I got more into the project and could see the scope and time commitment involved, I realized that I was in over my head. In the past, I might have ignored that and carried on because I had said I would, and I wouldn't have wanted to upset or disappoint people. But in this case, I knew that I needed to reevaluate the situation and say no.

I was able to forgive myself for not knowing ahead of time and give myself permission to renegotiate. I found a compassionate and honest way to share my experience and my needs. I helped them find a more suitable committee member, and we parted ways, with no hard feelings. Later on, one of the other members thanked me for being honest about my capacity and shared with me that they had a few nightmare stories about people who had agreed to help and said yes when they should have said no.

If your boundaries are too rigid, you will also have trouble connecting to your emotions. Sometimes we have boundaries that are too rigid, which makes it difficult for us to connect with people. To an empath, a person who uses boundaries as a kind of armor can feel robotic and heartless.

A healthy boundary is somewhere in the middle, not too loose and not too rigid. A healthy boundary is flexible, something we feel our way through moment by moment.

Let's look at how having a strong boundary makes you trustworthy and generates respect in other people.

## Good Boundaries Make You Trustworthy

Have you ever been on the receiving end when someone has said yes to you when they should have said no? It doesn't feel very good, and it can create tension and bad feelings in our relationships. We think that we are doing someone a huge service when we say yes, but if we don't actually mean it, it can lead to resentment and problems in our relationships.

Carmen was doing a fund-raiser for a local charity, and she asked her sister Jazmin, an empath, to help. For as long as they'd been sisters, Jazmin had always said yes to her big sister. Very soon, Jazmin was overwhelmed with the amount of work involved and started feeling resentful. It was too much work on top of Jazmin's already full life, and she did not share her sister's passion for this charity. Jazmin didn't want to disappoint Carmen, but she began to drop the ball on her part of the work. Saying yes but not following through created drama and a crisis in the project, and Carmen could not figure out why her sister was being so passive-aggressive. Carmen was confused and hurt by her sister's strange behavior and felt very sad that their normally tight connection was now fraught with bad feelings that Carmen didn't understand. Had she done something wrong? Why was Jazmin withdrawn and unhappy?

Soon the sisters were fighting, and the situation could have led to a permanent falling out. But Jazmin was studying boundaries, and one day she had a tearful heart-to-heart with Carmen. She confessed that she had never wanted to participate in the charity event and that she had said yes only to please her sister.

Carmen told Jazmin that it would have been fine to say no; in fact, it would have been a hundred times better than saying yes when she didn't mean it and then getting cranky, resentful, and passive-aggressive. The sisters worked out it and swore that from then on they would always be honest with each other about their yeses and nos. By getting clear about boundaries, they found a new level of trust with each other.

I want you to take that in. If you are lying with your yeses and nos, you are not trustworthy, and you are placing a burden on the people you are lying to. We can deeply trust people only if we can trust them to be honest about their yeses and nos. As with Carmen and Jazmin, not being honest about where our boundaries are can create an uncomfortable and unbalanced energy in our relationships.

# You Have Permission to Say No

Many empaths need permission to say no, at least in the beginning of their journey to empowerment. We are allowed to say no to anything that doesn't feel right to us, within reason. I am not talking about saying no to honoring your commitments; that is a vital part of our integrity, up to a point. But I am saying that we are allowed to say no to anything that threatens our safety or sense of self or is not in alignment with our well-being.

I recently worked with a twenty-year-old empath named Lexy whose was in an abusive relationship with an energy vampire. Lexy lived like a slave, cooking, working, doing housework, while her boyfriend slept all day, drank all night, and gambled heavily with any money that she brought home.

As she told her story, I asked her why she agreed to be treated this way. She looked at me blankly for a few minutes and then said that it had never occurred to her that she could say no. Lexy was raised in a highly religious and strict family where children were not allowed to say no to adults and women were discouraged from saying no to men. Her parents could not understand why she had run off with an older man; they had hoped that they had instilled better morals in her. But this was not a question of morality. Lexy was very unhappy with this situation, but it had never occurred to her that she could say no to it. Her parents had raised her to be passive and submissive, to not value herself. In fact, as a child, Lexy was punished whenever she said no, so she simply stopped saying it. She was so disconnected from her own will and her sense of self that she literally did not even think of saying no, even when an older, dominating man led her into a dangerous situation.

It took time—and a lot of therapy, healing work, and honest self-examination—for Lexy to begin to feel what she actually wanted, what she liked to do, how she felt about people, and where her boundaries were. Eventually Lexy learned to say yes *and* no to life as it unfolded around her. Her empowerment process led her to cut connections with both her family and the man she had run away with, and fortunately she had the inner strength and outer support she needed to learn how to set boundaries. And while Lexy's story may seem extreme, I share it with you an illustration of how sometimes empaths need permission to say no.

You have that permission, now and forever more.

Now let's take a look at two emotions that are vital in recognizing when we need to set a boundary.

## The Wisdom of Resentment and Anger

How do we know when we need to set a boundary? When we are not practiced in setting boundaries, we don't even know how to tell that we need to. Fortunately, our feelings of resentment and anger can give us the answer. Resentment is the emotion that we feel when we are over-giving in a relationship or situation and there is an energy imbalance. We feel resentful when we consistently give more than we receive.

Anger is also a great indicator that we need a boundary. Anger is a natural reaction when someone has stepped over our boundary in an energetic or actual trespass, or when a situation feels unfair and unjust.

If you have become disconnected from feeling your anger and resentment, you will miss these essential cues that alert you to boundary violations, so it's important to pay attention to and honor those feelings when they arise.

Here is a powerful exercise to help you connect with any resentful feelings. This will show you where you need to tighten up your boundaries.

## THE RESENTMENT INVENTORY

1. In your journal, write down a list of everything you feel resentful about in your life.

2. Include any relationship, work situation, or other situations and activities that you do. Let it all out and don't hold back.

3. Ask yourself what you need to do to reset the boundary in those situations.

It's good to notice any time you feel resentful and ask yourself what you need to do to have a healthier boundary for yourself.

Jason is a thirty-five-year-old dad who takes care of his three kids and manages the household while his wife, Linda, works a high-pressure job that involves a lot of travel. When he did his resentment inventory, he uncovered the fact that he was doing 90 percent of the housework, plus the food shopping, cooking, driving the kids around, taking care of the pets, and also tending to the couple's aging parents. He was also the assistant coach on his son's baseball team and handled more than his fair share of the organizing, fund-raising, and carpooling. The last straw happened when Jason allowed himself to be drafted into a church committee that he didn't have time for.

Jason was on the hairy edge of burnout, but he felt guilty complaining or asking his wife to do more at home. He knew she was also at her limit with her job and travel schedule. Doing the resentment inventory helped him see a pattern in his own behavior. He felt guilty that he wasn't earning the money, and every time Linda would complain about her stress levels, he would take on more responsibility, even if she wasn't asking him to.

Their family was headed for a breakdown, and they had even talked about separating, but Jason realized that it was up to him to ask for what he needed, to reset the boundary and to advocate for himself. He negotiated for a house-cleaning and laundry service, and they decided to use a delivery service for their groceries. Jason felt so happy and valued when Linda volunteered to help with the baseball team obligations, and the final piece of liberation came when Jason respectfully resigned from the church committee.

Jason used the resentment inventory to address the energy imbalances in his life to great effect. Thereafter, he would notice when he started to feel the faintest flicker of resentment and use that as an indicator that he needed to say no and manage his time and energy boundaries.

Now let's look at the emotion of anger as an equally powerful indicator.

Anger is an emotion that most empaths and spiritual people have difficulty with. We have a lot of judgments against being angry. Good, kind, spiritual people are not supposed to get angry, right?

But anger is a perfectly natural emotion; in fact, it is crucial to our empowerment. Anger is a key to making change in our lives. Plenty of spiritual people have been angry. Jesus, Gandhi, and Martin Luther King Jr. were all angry about social injustices, and they stand out as being committed to nonviolent expressions of that anger. That is something that we can all aspire to.

We feel angry when people are enslaved, oppressed, and exploited, so you should, too, if someone is attempting to exploit you as an individual or as part of a group.

The problem arises not from *feeling* anger, but from how most people *express* anger. We have all been witness to people who behaved very badly with their anger, lashing out with explosive rage or mean-spirited passive-aggressiveness. We may have an unhealthy pattern of internalizing anger, beating ourselves up. Or we may have been the victim of externalized anger in the form of bullying and even outright violence. We learn these behavior patterns from our parents, who model for us how to express our anger, and unfortunately many of them model destructive and dysfunctional ways to express anger.

Sadly, few of us are taught the value of anger and how we can express it in a clean and healthy way. I want to teach you how to express your anger in a healthy way so you can feel comfortable tapping into this empowering emotion, since it is one of the most powerful ways to know when you need to set a boundary. Appropriately channeled and expressed anger will also give you the energy and fuel that you need to take a stand for yourself.

We need to express our anger in ways that don't target ourselves or another person. Ideally, it needs to come out of our body in a productive and healthy way. When we turn our anger against ourselves, it leads to depression, addictions, and other self-destructive behaviors as well as stress and other health issues. When we target other people with our anger it leads to hatred, abuse, and violence in our relationships.

The solution is an *anger workout*. Here is how to do it.

## ANGER WORKOUTS

Anger loves to be expressed in physical ways. Think about what a child does when they are angry: they stomp, make fists, and yell. Anger wants to move through our voice, our hands, and our legs. Practice with these methods to find one that works for you.

- Journal your anger. Write it out as raw as you can; don't hold back. When you are done, if you feel you need to keep it private, rip it up or delete it.

- Get a punching bag and punch and kick it. Make sure you vocalize while you are doing that. Say *No!* Or scream and swear if you'd like to.

- In your car, turn the music up and scream, talk, shout, whine, complain, and curse. Let it all out. (If you're driving, keep your eyes on the road and drive safely!)

- Get a tennis racket or plastic baseball bat and whack your bed or couch with it. Make sure you breathe and vocalize while you do this. Saying *No* is always good, but let yourself voice your anger creatively.

- Take a boxing or kickboxing class. Running is also great for anger release.

- Get a dish or hand towel and wring the towel with your hands. Vocalize while you do this, say *No*, curse, or talk about what is angering you.

If you have a lot of built-up anger, I recommend that you do this at least once a day for five minutes a day as a minimum. This clears out stored anger in a healthy, nonviolent way.

Once we have learned productive, healthy ways to release our anger, it's more likely that we will allow ourselves to feel anger in the moment. Notice when anger comes up for you; it will show you where someone has crossed your boundary.

Now that we can see two powerful red flags that cue us in to when we need to set boundaries, let's look at some concrete and practical ways to do it.

## The Power of No

It's amazing that such a little word can cause such big problems. The word *no* carries a big emotional charge; in some cultures, families, and communities, it is a forbidden word and might be listed among the words one must never say in polite company. For many people, saying no to someone is the rudest thing you can do. We are taught that only really selfish people say no, and children are strongly discouraged from saying it to adults.

And yet, unless we want to be relegated to being compliant door-mats and fair game for users, abusers, and energy vampires, we must learn how to wield this most powerful of all words. Let's take a moment to unpack any baggage you might have around this word.

## MY RELATIONSHIP WITH NO

Take out your journal and write down any thoughts you have about the word *no*. Consider these questions.

- Were you allowed to say no when you were a child?

- What happened to you if you dared to say it? Was there backlash?

- Who was allowed to say it? Your mother or father, or both, or neither?

- At home, did no come out as rage or violence?

- How about in your school, place of worship, or other communities?

- What beliefs about your ability to say no are you still carrying from your childhood?

- Are those beliefs still serving you, or are you ready to let them go?

It's good to clear out any old beliefs that we have about this word and our right to say it. Now let's look at some different ways to own the power of no.

## Many Ways to Say No

There are many ways to say no that are socially acceptable, and for us as empaths it's important that find ways to say no that are both firm and also kind, polite, and compassionate. I recommend that you write down the ways that appeal to you and practice saying them in the mirror until they roll off your tongue with ease. I used to look myself in the eye in a mirror and practice saying them with a smile in my voice and a firmness in my belly. Here are some good ones:

- No thank you.

- Thank you for the kind offer, but I can't.

- I would so love to help you, but I am overcommitted right now and can't take on any new projects.

- I need to check my schedule and think about it. I'll get back to you in a day or two.

- I love what you are doing, and I appreciate your asking me, but I am not available.

- I am sorry, I can't right now. I will let you know if that changes.

A simple "no thank you" is my go-to phrase, especially in when confronted by pushy fundraisers who are counting on social pressure to squeeze a yes out of you. "How much would you like to donate? Ten, twenty, or fifty dollars?" is a common tactic, all of which can be washed away with a simple and courteous "No thank you." Use this phrase freely on anyone who is pushing anything on you—and be amazed at the results. One of my friends was about to be mugged in Miami. She was walking down the road outside her hotel when a man stopped in front of her and demanded her handbag. She said "No thank you!" and brushed past him. He stood gaping at her until she made it into her hotel safely.

Don't be surprised if you get some pushback from people when you start saying no, especially if they haven't heard that word from you very often. People will question your no and be offended, insulted, or angry. You may hear a lot of "How dare you say no to me?" It's okay to let that happen; it's inevitable, and people are entitled to their feelings too. If someone gives you some static about your newfound no, you can respond by saying something like "I am sorry you feel that way. My answer is still no." My children will tell you that one is very familiar to them! As we are retraining our people with our new no, there are bound to be some hard feelings. Let them have their feelings, as long as they are not abusing you, and stay firm.

When it comes to family, friends, and causes that are harder to say no to, I have learned to never give an answer to a request in the moment. I am too prone to say yes. As an empath, I truly feel what the other person needs, how they feel, and how big a deal it is for them. If I let myself, in the moment I will almost always say yes and then regret it. I have learned to say "Let me get back to you tomorrow." Then I think on it, usually while I am sitting by myself so that I can feel whether I am a yes or a no. I bring out my calendar and look at where I could fit it in. I consider whether or not it is in alignment with my mission or if it's a soul calling for me. Then I sleep on it and consider it again. After I have run it through all these filters, I will give an answer.

Once we are clear on our boundaries, we can also enlist help from other quarters. When my kids were younger, I told them that if they ever needed to say no to something, they could pin it on me. "No; my parents don't let me do that," or "No, I have to go home now; my mom is waiting for me."

I hope you find some much-needed power in that little word!

## Extreme Boundary Setting

Sometimes we need to hold a hard line with people and be willing to walk away from certain relationships. I call this *extreme boundary setting*, and although I hope you never find yourself in one of those situations, here are some guidelines to manage those very difficult boundaries. The key is to draw a line in the sand and be willing to walk away it you really need to. Here is an example.

I met Pranav in one of my workshops for empaths. He is a smart and sensitive young man who was trying to find a way to manage his energy around his strong-willed mother and aunts. His family had a plan for him and wasn't interested in what he wanted for himself, including the fact that he was dating a woman his mother didn't approve of. Pranav knew that if he was ever going to be happy and live his own life, he needed to set boundaries with his mother, and he was also clear that he did not want to totally step away from his family. Family ties were important to Pranav, but his mother and aunts came from a generation and culture vastly different from what Pranav was living.

"I know my mother loves me, but her expectations are about obedience and family duty. She believes that I should blindly follow her will. That doesn't work for me. She was raised in India, but I grew up here in the US, and here we have different needs and expectations."

Pranav decided how much time he was going to spend with his family. "Family dinner once a week and one phone call a week is what seemed right for me." Pranav explained to his mother that this was what he was going to do. "It was either that, or I was contemplating moving across the country," he told me.

His mother didn't like this rule, but as Pranav stayed firm and consistent with his new boundary, she gradually accepted it. Making a decision that worked for him and sticking by it helped Pranav feel empowered in the relationship rather than feeling like a victim.

The crisis came when his mother rejected the woman he was dating and began to plan an arranged marriage for Pranav.

"We had a showdown," he told me. "I refused to meet my mother and the prospective bride and told my mother that if she did not accept my girlfriend we would be moving from Boston to California and would be cutting ties with the family."

Pranav did not speak to his mother for almost a year, but when he announced his engagement, she came around.

Pranav's story shows how it is possible to choose where your boundary is. When we choose, we avoid feeling run over. Pranav knew it was a gamble, and he was fully prepared to cut ties with his family if they weren't willing to accept his terms. "I knew I was going to be okay either way and that I needed to be fully prepared to walk away." His story might have ended another way, but either way, he would have held onto his boundary.

## Cutting Ties

There are times when we need to cut people out of our lives completely. It's okay to do this, even if it goes against our cultural norms. Sometimes we find ourselves in situations so toxic that we must step away. Here are some times when you should cut ties with no hesitation:

- Any time there is physical or sexual abuse. It is never okay to allow yourself to be physically abused.

- The same holds true for emotional abuse. If someone is putting you down, yelling, blaming, telling you that you are crazy, humiliating you, or attempting to control you, that is abusive, and you need to end the relationship.

- When there is addiction that is not getting treated. It's is often necessary to cut ties with an active alcohol and drug abuser.

- We also need to leave behind relationships where are there are hate crimes and abuse based on our race, religion, sexual or gender orientation and our deepest identity and life choices.

- If you are being abused in a workplace, go through the appropriate human resource channels and report the abuse. If that doesn't resolve the issue, leave your job as soon as you can.

If you have to completely cut out your family, friends, or other people in your life, it's important to get support for yourself. Seek out therapy or a support group and find other people to help you fill the empty space. We can find our own spiritual families and other "families of choice" and create our own communities—and this can be an incredibly healing and nurturing experience.

## Getting Support for Those Extreme Cases

We might need external support to help us walk away from toxic relationships. If you feel physically or emotionally unsafe, it's crucial to get support. There are support systems all around us. Police, lawyers, and domestic violence advocates and shelters are here to help. If you feel threatened in any way, it's important to use these resources, many of which offer help free of charge. It's also likely that you will need emotional support, and there are therapists, support groups, shelters, and agencies that provide both temporary and long-term support for all kinds of situations.

When you need to set extreme boundaries, these are the essential steps:

- Find the conditions and boundaries that feel safe for you and explain them calmly.

- Be prepared to walk away from the relationship or situation if need be.

- If there is serious toxicity in the relationship and the person is not seeking help, then walk away.

- If you are in danger or feel a potential threat of danger, cut ties.

- Get support to help you process the experience.

- Create new friends and community to fill in the gap.

It's sad when you have to do this, but it's worth it to have a life full of people who love and respect you and your boundaries.

In our modern world, we have another potential ally for boundary setting: technology.

## Technology as an Energy Drain—or an Ally

Technology can be either an incredible asset for boundary setting or a debilitating drain on our energy. Television, smartphones, and especially social media can be energy sink holes for sensitives. The news channels stream constant images of pain and suffering, focusing on the things that are "newsworthy"—which most often means shocking and horrifying.

Social media can be fun and a great way to keep in touch with your friends, but it can also allow in energy designed to bring you down. It can give us such a fake and shallow look into other people's lives that when we compare our lives to the apparent lives of others, we feel not good enough. And so many people have experienced being cyberbullied at some point in their lives that it is a new epidemic, especially in the younger generations.

And smartphones put this all at our fingertips twenty-four hours a day. Texting and emails on your phone have blurred the boundary between work time and play time in an unhealthy way.

Remember, you are the boss of your technology; it is here to serve you, not the other way around. Having text, calling, email, and a hundred other connection-based apps all available on our phones 24/7 has given us a crazy idea that we should be available to everyone all the time.

Let me tell you, you don't have to be. It's a crazy, unhealthy idea. It's okay to unplug. I have gone so far as to delete the email app on my phone, which spends a lot of time in "do not disturb" mode, and that brings me great peace of mind.

Especially when you are an empath, it's vital to take media and technology breaks. Turn off the TV and your phone and go to places that have no WiFi; you will experience a kind of relief that we all need so badly. The world will still be there when you plug back in.

Our technology can also be a powerful tool for boundary setting. If you have difficult relationships with people, you can screen your calls. Don't answer your phone if you know it's an energy vampire on the other end. Let them leave a message and call them back tomorrow. Don't let people feel that you are at their beck and call. Clearly, if it's your friends, your lover, or your kids, be as available as you want to be; but for any tricky relationships, use your technology to create a buffer. Anything that isn't urgent and needs a boundary can wait at least twenty-four hours. The same goes for texts and emails.

My client Samantha was going through a rough divorce from a manipulative and cruel narcissist. She used all the technology she had to help create a buffer between them. She explained that she was not going to answer him directly and that he could leave a message on the phone or by text. If it was a civil message, she would respond the next day. If it was abusive, it was going to be relayed to her lawyer, who would respond in her stead—and she would be sending her soon-to-be ex the lawyer's bill.

She did the same with emails and also installed a closed-circuit camera at her front door, which stopped his bad behavior on her doorstep. Her ex tested this system a few times to see if she was serious, and when she stuck to her guns, he became reasonable and civil.

Consider what you might do to plug the energy leaks that overusing your tech can spring, and set a boundary for yourself for how much media you engage in. Then see if there are any places in your life where you can use tech to support your boundaries.

As you set out to master setting boundaries, you'll need to plan for what happens afterward. Learning to set boundaries can have an earthquakelike effect in yourself and in your life—and there can be aftershocks.

## It Will Feel Natural in Time

When you start setting boundaries, it's very common to feel guilty, ashamed, or afraid of the consequences. We empaths often feel like we are being a "bad" person when we set a boundary; it seems so mean and harsh when we are used to unquestioningly giving so much of ourselves to others. In setting boundaries, you are rewriting old scripts from your childhood about your level of self-worth and what constitutes a good person. It's normal to feel guilty and selfish, but it's important to work through those feelings and stick to your guns.

I hope that by now you see that being in a codependent relationship is not good for either party. Any relationship needs love and respect on both sides. By loving ourself deeply and putting ourself first in a relationship, we are giving the other person a choice to either respect our boundary or move on.

We also need to anticipate that other people may be angry or have an emotional reaction to our boundary. People are entitled to their feelings, but they should not be allowed to take it out on you. If rage, abuse, or violence is part of their expression, it's time to set another, firmer boundary on that. Practice what you need to say so that when the time comes you are ready and feel comfortable with the words.

"You are not allowed to speak to me that way. It's abusive, and I won't tolerate it." At that point hang up, walk away, or find another way to end the exchange. This is a good to time to allow your technology to create a boundary for you.

Absolutely expect that people will challenge you to see if you really mean it. Often they will up the ante and apply whatever pressure has worked in the past to see if you will cave in and go back to your former pattern. They will run through all the manipulations they know; they might whine and complain, pull the victim card, try to guilt or shame you, then escalate to bullying and possibly even abuse or violence. You don't have to put up with any of that. You are under no obligation to help them process that or fix it for them in any way unless they are being civil and you choose to engage in that conversation with them.

Keep in mind that to be emotionally healthy, you must choose to not caretake their feelings or fall back into codependency. And any escalating bad behavior will require that you set another boundary. Do not apologize, waiver, or overly explain yourself. Be calm, clear, and consistent. Wavering, explaining, and apologizing all send a mixed message and show them you are not really serious about this. They don't have to like it or even understand it, really—they just have to do it.

It's worth all that work, since they will either choose to respect your new boundary, which will help both of you, or choose to walk away, which may also be the best possible outcome.

This is a difficult process that can shake you to your core, so if you need help, get it. This kind of work challenges our childhood programing for what we needed to do to survive. So for some it can bring up tremendous anxiety. It may feel like a matter of life and death. But support is all around us, in the form of therapists, support groups, spiritual communities, and so many other options.

I have seen empaths use couples and family therapists to great effect in helping family members decide on healthy boundaries together and what to do when someone slips a boundary. It's very useful to talk about it and discuss the potential consequences together in advance. Have a family meeting or a couple's relationship conversation and talk it through at a time when everyone is more or less centered and not feeling defensive. And if you can't get there, get help from a third party.

We are not seeking perfection here. It's okay to try, make mistakes, and feel your way through it. It's a skill that takes a lot of practice, so feel free to try and try again. The effort that you are putting in here is worth every second, and the payoffs are huge. For me, establishing boundaries has allowed me to step into the world and do the work I do without a lot of fear and anxiety. I feel fairly confident in my ability to handle difficult people and situations, and I have a baseline level of trust in myself that gives me a kind of freedom to be in the world and take risks.

You deserve to have a life full of loving relationships with people who respect and honor you, and it can be yours when you simply say no.

# CHAPTER 6

# Exchanging Energy in Romance, Sex, and Love Without Losing Ourselves

Love and sex are two of the most powerful human experiences. We are at the mercy of these twin desires, and in many ways they become the foundation of our lives. Our yearning for love and the sexual expression of it seems to have the power to bring us either to heaven or to hell.

We are at our most open and most vulnerable in our sexual relationships, so we need a deep understanding of how to manage our energy and our boundaries. During our intimate moments with another person, we open our bodies, our hearts, and our souls in ways that can make us defenseless. In the hands of someone who loves, reveres, and respects us, we can find bliss and transcendent joy. When we find ourselves at the mercy of an energy vampire, we can feel ripped open, trapped, and desperate.

This is true for most humans, but especially for empaths. We struggle with how we absorb energy from others and how we set boundaries, so adding the powerful energies of love and sex to the mix can up the ante considerably. Having a sexual relationship with someone, even a very casual one, can alter our energy field and create energetic and emotional attachments with that person that we need to be mindful of. A powerful energy exchange happens during sexual encounters, but we are often unconscious of this, and we can easily be drained by our lovers.

In this chapter we will discover what happens to our biochemistry, our bodies, and our energy fields when we engage in sexual activity with another person. And we'll learn how to manage and maximize our energy during this special activity, as well as how to create healthy boundaries with our lovers. This also means knowing how to clear up old relationships and lingering emotional and energetic connections with our past lovers.

Let's begin by taking a look at what happens when we fall in love.

## Empaths in Love

Falling in love is an incredibly soulful experience that often defies logic and the rules of society, and we are not the same person that we were on the other side of that love affair, even if it ends in heartbreak. If you have ever been transcendently changed by a love affair, you know what I am talking about.

There is a mystical, soulmate aspect to love relationships that all empaths yearn for, yet what we usually get is an object lesson in how to manage our boundaries. David Schnarch, author of *Passionate Marriage: Keeping Love and Intimacy Alive in Committed Relationships*,[10] says that committed relationships are "people growing machines" whose function is to bring up opportunities for personal and spiritual growth. Happiness happens along the way, but it is in the pursuit of intimacy— allowing another person to truly know us—that we really grow. And our current primary relationship allows us to work through deeper and deeper levels of our childhood wounding.

At some deep archetypal level, we yearn to merge with this other person, to truly surrender to another. We become vulnerable to another person and open ourselves to them on every level of our being. When that person doesn't have our best interests at heart or is incapable of truly loving and giving to someone else, we open ourselves to a world of hurt.

In general, empaths are highly committed to their primary relationships. We are relational beings and need relationships on so many levels. Of course, many empaths have wonderful, supportive, and healthy relationships, but many more struggle to find peace and empowerment in this part of life. When it doesn't go well, empaths tend to become codependent, giving too much of ourselves to our relationships. And we can easily fall prey to the idea that our powerful and healing love can fix our partner.

Our primary relationships are generally a reflection of the energy and relationship dynamics in our family of origin when we are very young children. These energy patterns get formed deep in our hearts and our psyches, and we learn to recognize what "love" is based on our parent's relationships to each other and to their young children.

We then are attracted to primary love relationships based on these old patterns. No wonder these relationships are often so difficult. And we tend to also drag in lifetime patterns from our past lives, which also need clearing and usually mirror and amplify what happened to us as children. We can also be heavily impacted by our *legacy wounds*—injuries and issues that live in the psyche of our entire lineage, from our great-grandparents down to us.

So most of us have a full plate of unresolved issues that need healing, and since we can't do anything about this patterning when we are little and becoming imprinted with it, we choose as partners people we hope will give us opportunities to heal these wounds.

Through recent centuries, marriage and relationship paradigms have been shifting away from the survival-based tribal relationships of our ancestors. In the past, marriage was about mutual survival, and the needs of the group outweighed the needs of the individual.

Many empaths reject the traditional marriage paradigm in search of a new kind of relationship. Ideally, we learn the essential skills that we need to have a *conscious relationship* or *spiritual partnership*. In these types of relationships, we consciously use the relationship to confront our issues and work through them with our partners without blaming them for our own triggers and projections.

It's not all bad, of course. Our partnerships bring us so much joy too. We create children and homes together; we stick with each other through good times and bad. And there is much joy possible in sharing a life with someone, as well as the deep growth possibility in sharing a conscious relationship.

## Empath Relationship Patterns

Empaths long for a close relationship with their partner and have the potential to make fantastic partners, since we all have natural emotional intelligence and a strong desire to bond with another. But we need to watch out for these common patterns and pitfalls:

- Codependency is a big problem for empaths. To feel okay, we need our people to be okay.

- Most empaths hate being single and will sometimes jump too quickly into a new relationship just to avoid feeling lonely.

- Since empaths orient our identity around our relationships, we tend to hold on to a relationship longer than we should.

- In the most extreme cases, we become relationship addicts, giving up our own self to preserve a relationship is that not healthy for us.

- Dating can be a painful emotional and energetic trap. Most empaths love being in a relationship but hate the dating scene and will do almost anything to get out of it or hurry through it, making a premature exclusive commitment.

- Empaths can be easily seduced by someone claiming to be their soulmate, as they crave that connection more than anything.

- Our compassionate and spiritual nature can see the good in everyone and connect to the soul-level potential of a person— and then be really surprised when the person's personality disappoints.

All of these traits and tendencies can make us extra vulnerable to the energy vampires, users, and abusers of the world who sniff out these "weaknesses" and easily use them against us. Fortunately, we have the potential of healthy self-esteem and good boundaries to come to the rescue!

Now that we have explored some of the basics of how empaths do in love relationships, let's talk about this alluring idea of finding a soulmate. Empaths love the idea of a soulmate and often spend their whole life searching for these deep and mystical connections. Let's take a look at this specific kind of relationship and the impact it can have on us, as well as sort through some of our misconceptions about what a soulmate really is.

## The Soulmate Quest

It may be that empaths long for soulmate relationships more than other people do. Because empaths are highly spiritual old souls, we have an unusually strong ability to sense the soul energy of another person. We also are more finely tuned to our past lives and the soul-level connections with others.

We can sniff out a possible soulmate a mile away, and we have a true need to connect with our soulmates. Yet we carry many myths and misconceptions about the soulmate process. The Hollywood and Disney ideal of a soulmate relationship has made us believe that we are meant to fit together in blissful harmony and live happily ever after. In this fantasy soulmate relationship, there is only one other person in the whole world who is meant for you, and you fit together like a lock and key. This perfect other is your destiny, and once you meet, somehow they will magically fulfill of all of your needs. Your soulmate will be able to read your mind, know what you need on every level of your being, and provide that for you. Your soulmate will be loyal and faithful and never leave you, for all of eternity.

According to this myth, we are longing for the "you complete me" movie ideal of a relationship, in which we don't need to work on the incompletely healed parts of ourselves because our perfect other provides that for us. I have seen many empaths stick with very unhealthy relationships, using the soulmate ideal as an excuse. And sadly, there are just as many new age-y empaths who throw away perfectly wonderful partners in the quest for their "twin flame."

Psychologists say that the desire for this type of soulmate arises out of an infantile need to merge with a loving parent who meets all our needs completely. Metaphysicians, theologians, and philosophers trace our soulmate obsession back to our fundamental desire to regain union with the source of life.

While all of that is part of the desire to fully merge with a soulmate, and although most soulmate relationships spark incredible growth in us, they don't automatically have a traditional happy ending. And soulmates come in many different forms. Whether it's a romantic partner, a life companion, a teacher, or a treasured friend, a real soulmate relationship will help us grow and transform in powerful ways. Growth and transformation is the point and the potential in our real soulmate connections.

We don't have just one soulmate, that one perfect other, as far as I can tell. We have a soul *family* with whom we go through our cycle of incarnation. The idea that we have a one and only isn't practical, since we need many kinds of relationships in order to grow. I have not seen much evidence of the "twin flame," that one perfect other described by some as one soul dividing into two who are reunited here on earth. In the thirty years that I have been seeing clients, I have seen this only once—and it was twin sisters who had a rather tortured relationship with each other.

Your real soulmates are the people in your life you couldn't get rid of even if you wanted to. They might be your parents and siblings, your children, your spouses and your exes. Even the people who torment and abuse us are often our soulmates—they fall into a special category of soulmates that the Buddhists call the *noble friends*. They present us with an adversarial relationship in which our growth comes through friction. These challenging soulmates bring us the opportunity to grow much as an effective Marine drill sergeant makes a good soldier.

We create an unwritten agreement known as a *soul contract* with members of our soul family for our mutual growth. The contracts are always mutually beneficial, with the potential for both people to grow, as we saw in the potential for growth between an empath and an energy vampire.

Empaths almost always recognize these people when we meet them. If you have ever been sucked into a relationship that seems amazing at first and then went sour, you might be feeling the pull of the soul contract between you. It's very hard to walk away from a soul contract, although we can, since this is a free will dimension.

Romantic soulmates come in at least two different flavors. There is the passionate, highly romantic type that most of us think about when we imagine a soulmate. I always think of these as the *face-to-face* soulmate, since we experience such powerful and immediate intimacy with these people. One of my colleagues jokingly calls these the *in your face* soulmates—also a good descriptor. These relationships are characterized by incendiary sexual chemistry, the sensation of falling in love instantly and feeling magnetically connected to that person. This type of soulmate relationship tends to burn hot and quickly, and its purpose is to challenge us and create rapid, soul-level growth in us.

Often there is a clash of wills, as hot sexual chemistry alternates with passionate fighting. Although we long to hold onto this type of erotic love, it usually burns out quickly, leaving us a changed person. The potential lessons here will vary from person to person, but it's often about boundary setting and learning to maintain our own sense of self in a powerful relationship.

Here is a beautiful story that illustrates all that is possible between two face-to-face soulmates.

Deborah is an empath, an energy healer, life coach, and psychologist. Her story showcases the incredible potential for transformation that an empath can find in a love affair. She met her partner, Lucia, at a conference for psychologists. They had an immediate and intense connection.

"Lucia was my soulmate—I knew it the minute that I saw her," Deborah told me. "It felt as though we were pulled together like magnets; we literally couldn't stay away from each other. We spent the first hour that we met trying to figure out if we had actually met before, because it felt like we recognized each other."

There were a lot of challenges in their relationship right from the beginning. They had to navigate living on opposite coasts, and a cultural and age difference between them, since Lucia was from Brazil and living in California, while Deborah was a lifelong New Yorker.

Deborah found that she was the one who compromised and accommodated, giving up ground to keep the couple together. "It's amazing how you make assumptions that because you love someone you have the same values, agendas, and needs. And then you find out the hard way that you don't."

Within six months of meeting, the couple had married, moved in together, and started the process of having children. But once they settled into daily life, cracks in the foundation of their relationship started to appear.

"Lucia needed to be in an open relationship," Deborah told me. "She traveled a lot and loved to spontaneously connect with people. I am not sure how I missed this about her, but one day it dawned on me that she had lovers, both men and women, everywhere she went."

Deborah was heartbroken but worked hard to keep the family together, mostly by accommodating. Eventually she found that she needed to set boundaries and say how she felt. After trying to make it work for years, Deborah had to acknowledge that being in an open relationship didn't work for her. She craved a deeper level of trust and commitment than Lucia could provide. She concluded, "Lucia is a wonderful, talented, and beautiful person, and there is nothing wrong with the way she needs to live. It just doesn't work for me."

During the hardest parts of the relationship, Deborah said, "I felt gutted, like I totally lost myself. I gave up everything that was important to me to try and keep the relationship and the family going. I felt that I needed her like oxygen, and that if she was my one and only soulmate, my twin flame, then I would never find another partner.

"I thought I was going to get a 'happily ever after' soulmate relationship. Instead, I got a soulmate who created more growth in me than any other person has ever done. I learned where my boundary was and also how to speak up about it and advocate for my own needs. I learned that I could endure heartbreak and a breakup and still thrive. I learned that I love myself enough to not give up my core self to another person, and that happiness doesn't come from another person but from honoring and loving myself. And I learned that I am basically a monogamous person who needs that container in order to feel safe in a relationship. I learned a lot!"

Deborah and Lucia both put in a lot of effort to try and make their relationship work, but eventually they parted ways. They continued to be friends and coparents to their two children, and they both eventually found happiness with new partners who better reflected their core relationship needs.

The other type of soulmate is more of a companion or life partner. These relationships usually start out as friendships that evolve into something more. Although they don't have the same fiery sexual passion and chemistry as the other type, they are more comfortable and tend to be long lasting. It's as if two people are standing shoulder to shoulder, holding hands and working together in life toward mutual goals, such as raising a family or running a business together. These *shoulder-to-shoulder* soulmates can teach us about the power of compassion, long-lasting commitment, and the joy of achieving mutual goals together.

And we also have soulmates who are more like sparring partners. This often arises from the empath/narcissist dynamic that we discussed in chapter 4. It can be very difficult to reconcile the reality of an abusive relationship with someone who is a soulmate, but my clients have described this situation. From the soul's perspective, we can be working through the same difficult dynamic with a soulmate over the course of a few different lifetimes, returning to the same person over and over again. This can give us the practice and opportunity that we need to work through our most challenging relationships lessons.

Liam, a gentle-hearted empath, was working through a difficult relationship with his wife, a strong-willed warrior type person. Liam had known it was a soulmate connection from the moment they met. They married right after college, and after a brief honeymoon stage the couple went into a long period of power struggle. Although Katrina had a very self-aware, spiritual side, she could also be domineering, controlling, and mean. Liam struggled to find his power in the relationship. The breakthrough came when the two of them, sharing a common interest in spiritual growth, attended a past-life regression workshop together.

Although they were doing separate meditations, both of them recalled the same lifetime, which had taken place in ancient Egypt. Liam had been a mistreated slave and Katrina a cruel slave owner who did not value the lives of her slaves. They had been incarnating together since then, trying to ease the painful karma between them. On a soul level, Katrina needed to make amends for her cruel treatment of Liam and to learn empathy and compassion for others. Liam needed to find his power and sovereignty. He needed to find ways to say no, to advocate for himself and, if necessary, to walk away from a marriage that was not healthy for him.

It took them a while to process all the implications of this knowledge, but eventually they had a conversation in which Katrina acknowledged her controlling behavior and emotional cruelty to Liam in this lifetime. She apologized and asked him what she needed to do to make amends. Liam was finally able to ask for what he needed and share his experience of being with her. Eventually, with the help of a couples counselor, they were able to find a mutually beneficial and loving relationship with each other.

Let's consider how we can recognize our soulmates when we meet them.

## Recognizing Our Soulmates

Empaths are highly tuned in to the concept of a soulmate and often long for one. While other people can easily meet random people and form good relationships with them, empaths seem to need a soulmate connection for their primary relationships. Here are some ways that we recognize our soulmates:

- An instant feeling of connection, of having known each other before

- Immediately trusting the other person and moving through the stages of commitment and connection very quickly

- Feeling a magnetic attraction to the other person

- Seeing a light in their eyes or around their head

Remember: a soulmate doesn't guarantee you a happily ever after! But a soulmate does guarantee growth.

While we are discussing empaths in love, we need to address empaths' propensity to see only the good in a person while ignoring their more difficult aspects.

## Soul Versus Personality

As empaths, we are naturally wired to feel other people on a soul level. It seems as if we see others through rose-colored glasses, but I think it's deeper than that. We experience people on the level of the soul and sometimes remember them from past lives.

The core essence of our soul doesn't change much from lifetime to lifetime, even though the circumstances of our lives and our bodies do. Our core essence contains enduring elements such as compassion, love, generosity, or leadership. And it also contains our life purpose, which might be a desire to be a caretaker—or a visionary.

The *personality* is the egoic part of us that contains our quirks and the individual variations of this lifetime. Maybe it's a sense of humor, or a mean streak, or anxiety, or a vulnerability to addiction. We can also think of the soul as the super-conscious or higher self and the personality as the ego self.

The tricky thing for empaths is that because we are old souls, there is a strong coherence between our personality and our soul. Because the soul and the personality match, we are pretty much "what you see is what you get." When someone has coherence between soul and personality, we experience them as being very soulful and having a high level of integrity.

New and middle soul people are more likely to have a divergence. Their personality may be very different from their soul. This is normal for soul development, but it is very confusing to empaths. We feel a person's soul, and maybe we remember it from a past-life relationship, so we wonder why they are acting in a way that is not like their soul essence at all.

It's important, when you are choosing a partner, to look at the total person, including their personality quirks. It's hard to have a happy or functional relationship when you are wishing they would live up to the potential that you know is there rather than the challenging personality you are dealing with every day.

Empaths need to let go of the tendency to choose from that soul level, seeing the person's potential and ignoring the troublesome personality. We are a unique combination of our core soul essence as well as our personality, and both must be considered.

Let's take a look at what happens to our energy field during sexual encounters so that we know how to manage our energy and avoid the pitfalls that can happen when we don't.

## The Energetics of Sexuality

Sex opens us to each other in a way that no other human activity does. We exchange energy, pleasure, breath, and body fluids with our beloved. As lovers, we find ways to literally enter into each other's bodies as well as touch each other's hearts and souls. The potential for joy, healing, and growth is tremendous. Mystics and metaphysicians say that sex and death are the two greatest initiators into the world of transcendent experiences. Both push us to the very edge, and perhaps over the edge of known experiences and can connect us to our own divinity.

We already know that our energy field is dynamic and ever changing, always a snapshot of how we are feeling and what we are doing in the moment. Sexual activity can light up our energy field, flooding it with extra energy. During sex, we open up, both releasing and absorbing a tremendous amount of psychic, physical, and emotional energy.

Ideally, we choose partners who share love, kindness, and respect with us, in which case our energy field and our whole being receive a boost of healing and enlightening energy. In the worse cases we engage in unhealthy relationships with people, sharing disrespect, thoughtlessness, and even harmful and hateful energy, which will damage our energy fields.

Be mindful of who you let into your being in this way, and honor the sacred energy exchange that is possible here. If you choose partners who are either disconnected or hurtful to you, expect to pay the price in your energetic system too.

For many empaths, casual sex is not an empowering choice. If that is true for you, it's important to honor that about yourself, even in our current culture, where casual sex is in vogue, especially among young people. Therefore, part of having safe sex will require that you keep your heart safe, too, by choosing lovers who will treat you with loving kindness and respect.

Let's consider how sex and orgasm actually create an emotional and energetic bond with our lovers.

## Oxytocin, the Lovers' Bond

When we have an orgasm, many amazing things happen in our body and our brain. There is a release of the neurotransmitter oxytocin, which floods our brain with a feeling of love, connection, and wellbeing. It's also released when we hug someone, and in both mother's and baby's brains during nursing. Oxytocin is part of the reason we tend to fall in love with sexual partners. Evolution has created a natural bond between sexual partners and their offspring, an evolutionary adaptive strategy helpful to the survival of the human species. Sex often leads to babies, and babies survive when both parents bond with each other and the baby. This is the magic of oxytocin.

If you want to increase the emotional bond with your lover, continue to hold them and gaze at each other for at least twenty minutes after an orgasm, since that is the peak time that oxytocin affects our brain chemistry.

In addition to the bliss of oxytocin, an orgasm creates a rush of the life force energy, also called *kundalini energy*. When we have a healthy and open energy field, sexual activity stimulates a rush of kundalini energy that starts at the perineum and floods up our spine, clearing and healing our energy centers as it goes. At the peak of our climax, it floods the heart energy center, opening and clearing it, then goes all the way up the spine, opening the pineal gland and erupting out of the crown energy center.

When this kundalini energy is allowed to flow all the way up the spine, both men and women experience heart-opening, soul-filling, full-body orgasms.

Before the heart is fully open, the kundalini energy will recycle through the sexual energy center without rising up the spine. This kind of orgasm is more physical and genitally focused, and the energy release is less profound. Still delightful, but short of the full potential. It's possible to learn specific breathing techniques to use during sex that move the energy up the spine and recirculate it through our energy field— techniques that practitioners of tantra have known for centuries.

When we learn how to breathe freely through an orgasm and allow the kundalini energy to rise through us, we can use this to clear and heal our own energy fields as well as bring us more heart- and soul-opening pleasure. Empaths often figure out on their own that heart-connected sex is one of the best ways to heal and clear their energetic systems.

# ENERGY CIRCULATING BREATH

This is one of the most powerful and most basic sacred sexuality techniques. It helps you move the sexual energy up from the genitals and into the heart and crown energy centers. As sexual energy builds, many of us tend to hold our breath, which reduces the intensity of the experience. Breathing in long, slow, deep breaths calms the nervous system and helps your mind focus on pleasure—and, in case you suffer from a wandering mind during sex, on your partner. Slowing your breathing down will delay orgasm and keep your energy building for as long as you want it to.

1. During sex, focus on slowing your breath rate.

2. Try using the four-count breathing technique: breathing in for four counts and exhaling for four counts.

3. If that is easy for you, stretch it out to seven or eight counts.

4. Experiment with breathing from the base of your spine, up your spine and out the top of your head.

5. When you orgasm, don't hold your breath; let your breathing continue naturally.

6. If you hold eye contact with your partner and breathe with them, you will increase the pleasure and shared connection.

Now that we have discussed the power of breathing and your brain chemistry, let's talk about something else that all empaths and energetically sensitive people need to know. It's a little weird to talk about it, but it is so important to understand the impact of sharing body fluid with our sexual partners.

# Swapping Energy During Sex

All body fluids hold a psychic and energetic imprint of the person who produced them. Blood, in particular, holds the psychic and energy imprint, the energy signature of the person that it belongs to. Blood is a highly charged substance—literally the liquid form of our life force energy. The same is true for our other body fluids, including semen, saliva, and amrita. (Amrita, originally a term for immortality or the nectar of immortality, also refers to female ejaculate.)

When we exchange these fluids with each other during sex, we are exchanging energy at the deepest levels. We literally absorb these substances into our body, and because they have such a strong psychic and energetic imprint, we are absorbing their energy at the deepest level that we can.

I believe that on top of a general psychic imprint of a person, body fluids (sweat, tears, saliva, menstrual blood, bile, ejaculate, urine) can also contain uncleared energy residue—the lingering leftover emotional and psychic residue picked up in the course of daily living. Fulfilling sexual exchanges can help us to release and clear this residue.

It's important to learn how to transmute the sexual energy we receive from our partner—otherwise we can be stuck with it. We can use a breathing meditation to help transmute and clear this energy.

Yvonne needed to learn to transmute the sexual energy she received from her partner. Yvonne is a highly sensitive empath who also works as a medical assistant in a nursing home. She is also an artist with a growing reputation. She and her partner, Anthony, a police officer, live in a big East Coast city. They each enjoy the way that they serve others, yet it takes a toll on them to be working in such highly charged psychic environments as well as living in a city with all kinds of energy constantly running through it.

Yvonne noticed that she was very sensitive to Anthony's energy, especially when he came home from work. Anthony always knew he felt better after being intimate with Yvonne, so it was often the first thing he wanted to do after coming home from a work shift. But Yvonne felt as if she was absorbing all the pain and trauma that Anthony released during sex.

Yvonne studied sacred sexual practices and learned how to breathe, bring in the light, and transmute the energy that Anthony was releasing. It was so powerful that Anthony learned the same practices, holding Yvonne's gaze and breathing into his heart, so that he could help Yvonne release and clear her energy too.

Together, they were able to lift each other up to new heights. Their lovemaking was more loving, blissful, and pleasurable than ever. And they noticed that they were reaping the benefits of this mutually generated energy in other areas of their lives. Anthony was promoted at work, and Yvonne became more and more creative, her paintings selling in galleries all over New England.

Sexual energy is life force energy. It can be consciously generated and used to create miracles in our lives. And it can also wreak havoc if we are not careful. Besides the energy exchange of sexual encounters, we also must be aware of leaving more permanent energy connections with our lovers in the form of energy cords.

## Energy Cords

When we have a strong connection with another person, these connections exist on every level; they are emotional and psychic and can also be found in our energy fields. These types of connections can be experienced in our energy fields as *energy cords*, perceived psychically as strings or ropes of energy that connect us to another person. Though energy cords are not seen with your eyes, you can experience their effects.

Empaths are frequently aware of the cords that connect them with others. We feel them as a physical pulling, tugging, or pushing sensation in our bodies, or a strong psychic and emotional connection with the other person. If you have a cord with someone, you might dream about them and get empathic hits of what that person is feeling and thinking. If you are corded to an energy vampire, they will use this psychic and energetic link to drain your energy even when you are not with them.

It's possible to have this type of connection with anybody, even in a casual relationship. However, the more long-term and intense the relationship, the stronger and deeper the cord. When we fall in love, we form a cord that goes from heart to heart. Lovers can form cords with each other even after only one sexual connection. Cords with our sexual partners connect us through the sexual energy center. We can also have psychic cords that connect from the third eye, which allow us to connect to the other person psychically.

Parents can have energy cords with their children; friends can have cords with friends, and even a brief interaction with someone can create a cord if it carries enough emotional charge. If, long after an encounter happened, you are still thinking about that person who cut you off in traffic or the heated exchange you had with someone in a store, you may have formed a cord with them.

If you are working in the service industry, you may form cords with the people you are working with. I see them on nurses, teachers, and massage therapists. Anyone in the helping professions should do regular cord clearing, ideally through a daily ritual of grounding, clearing, and protecting. I once cleared dozens of cords off a sex worker who really cared about his clients.

If you are thinking a lot about one of your clients or students long after the work day is over, that's a sure sign there is a cord between you. Cords form when we have an expectation that we can and should help or save someone. When we connect energetically in our attempt to take away someone's pain, we form a cord. When our client, student, or patient has an expectation that we will save or fix them, they will attach a cord to us, and if we buy into the idea that we are supposed to save them, we will let them.

Cords go both ways; no one can create a cord to us unless the energy flows through it in both directions. So on some level you have allowed each cord connection and probably helped to create it. This means you are responsible for cleaning up any problematic cord—and not blaming the other person for it. It's very important to acknowledge imbalanced cords—that is, cords through which one person is drawing more energy than the other is—and clean those up too.

*Light cords* happen very naturally when we love someone. These are made of light and represent the positive emotional connection that we have with our people. When I perceive these psychically, they look like beautiful, glowing fiber-optic cables connecting two people. These cords are normal, natural, and full of love and don't need to be cleared.

But when a relationship ends, we need to clean up the cord with our lovers by resolving any unprocessed issues; cords can't be removed by force of will or out of anger.

Cords become problematic when we have unresolved emotions and issues with other people. Anger, grief, and jealousy clog up the light cords and make them dark, heavy, and unhealthy. In a codependent relationship—in which we have a powerful need, expectation, or unhealthy attachment to a person or their behavior, not fully based in love—the cord becomes a problem and needs to be cleared.

Now that we know about energy cords, what do we need to do to clear them?

---

## QUICK CORD CLEARING MEDITATION

This is a great meditation to add to your daily practice; it will help keep your energy field clear from the more casual cords that we form with people. You will know you have a cord that needs clearing if you are thinking about a person repetitively, or going over and over a conversation in your head, and you can't get that person out of your mind.

1. Begin with the basic grounding, clearing, and protective bubble meditation that you learned in chapter 3.

2. Visualize the person that you thinking about. Imagine that they are standing in front of you.

3. Ask or imagine that they are surrounded by light and fully supported by all the resources that they need—and that you are too.

4. Notice whether you can see, feel, or perceive the cord that is connecting the two of you. Acknowledge that you allowed the cord to form and that the energy is going both ways through the cord.

5. Give yourself some time to feel your feelings and express what you need to express to the other person. Use this time to take responsibly for your part in the cord.

6. Ask the cord to evolve to its highest form. Sometimes it will evolve into a light cord at this point.

7. If the cord is resistant, imagine that you can use a sword or some other tool to cut through it. I like the light saber from Star Wars; it's clean and cauterizes as it goes. Use the sword to cut the cord.

8. Try setting an intention that the two of you will find your highest and best relationship, and let go as much as you can. Send them a well wish and release them.

9. Finish with a few grounding breaths.

Deeper cords with our soulmates, family members, and lovers need a different approach, which we will work through later in this chapter.

There are some other kinds of cords that are more destructive and harder to clear—cords based more on our need to control someone else or their need to control us. There are several types: *hooks* and *trackers*.

## Hooks

A hook looks exactly like it sounds: a cord with big hook on the end. Hooks form between people who have an unhealthy, controlling relationship. They present a problem that must be addressed.

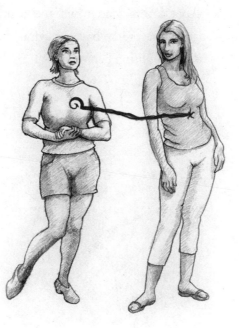

I see hooks in people who have an abusive, controlling, and demanding relationship; for example, an energy vampire might have a hook into an empath. The hook is the place where the empath is letting themselves be controlled by allowing themselves to feel guilty or by being manipulated. While cords can be cleared or evolved, hooks must be removed. It is possible to do this yourself with the cord clearing practice we just learned. If that doesn't work, try working with an energy healer to get it done.

## Trackers

Since our sexual relationships with people are so powerful and so primal, we really leave a strong energetic imprint with each other. *Tracker* is the term applied to the cords that form with our lovers. I see these psychically as a small energetic object, about the size and shape of a die, in the sexual energy center, located in the navel area. Trackers are used to keep track of our lovers, and when the relationship is not healthy, this can lead to some pretty bad behavior, such as extreme jealousy, possessiveness, and stalking behaviors.

I dated an energy vampire for a time. In the beginning I enjoyed his psychic connection to me. He was one of the most psychic people that I had ever met. He always knew when something was wrong in my life or if I was upset. He would show up out of the blue when I needed him, because he felt like something was off, and he would be right. It was all good, until it wasn't. He was also a very jealous and a predatory energy vampire. He didn't like it when I had connections with other people. As our relationship was ending, his tracking stopped feeling supportive and protective and started becoming scary and intrusive. He used that energetic connection to actually stalk me until I went to my energy healer, who removed the tracker that my lover had installed in me.

If someone installs a tracker in you, they will not only know where you are and how you are feeling, but they may well get intense psychic hits about you or feel what you are feeling, just like an empath.

So, knowing about these kinds of energetic attachments that we have with other people, let's learn how to clean them up.

## Clearing Unhealthy Attachments

It's important to recognize and clear these unhealthy attachments with other people. However, I don't believe in an angry slash-and-burn cord clearing, since that isn't effective.

Since it takes two people to form a cord, when you resolve your own feelings and allow yourself to express your emotions, needs, and desires in a healthy way, the cord will take care of itself. So when we resolve the emotional tangle we have with another person, a cord will usually clear on its own or transform into a lighter cord. However, the darker cords, which stem from an unresolved emotional tangle, need an active intervention.

There are healers who will cut these or yank them out of you, sort of like pulling weeds out of the ground. Sometimes that is necessary. I favor a more natural process, about healing things within our own self, saying what we need to say, and setting our boundaries. When we get matters right inside of us, there is no need to mess with the other person, especially not in anger.

I once did an energy healing session on a young man named Trevor. He had studied Reiki and taken some energy healing classes, so he knew all about energy cords. Trevor came to me complaining that try as he might, he could not clear the cords between himself and his ex-girlfriend, who had left him for another person. Trevor was still extremely angry at his ex. He was in full blame-and-complain mode and hadn't yet looked at whatever contributing factors he had added to the breakup. He was feeling victimized, hurt, and very angry.

I could see the cord between the two of them: it was pulsing with anger and hurt that he was sending toward his ex. He was still using it to send her a lot of angry and hurt energy. No wonder he hadn't been able to clear it! I had no doubt that she would experience this as an energy whammy almost on the level of a psychic attack.

Trevor was attempting to clear the cord by slashing away at it with an imaginary sword or burning it with fire. He couldn't understand it when the cord would pop right back even after all that slashing and burning. And he wasn't yet willing to acknowledge that there was a part of him still struggling to let her go that was punishing her for the pain she had caused him.

When I looked deeper at his energy field, I saw an older, thicker, and very dark cord that went from his solar plexus to his mother. As Trevor began to work through his pain and anger, the cord to his ex-partner lightened up. He did anger workouts (see chapter 5) and cried a lot in our sessions to release the grief he was feeling. Over the course of a few months, Trevor began to connect the breakup with his ex to the painful abuse he had experienced as a child at the hands of his mother.

Trevor realized that his ex was a stand-in for his mother and that he had projected a lot of his neediness and pain into that relationship. He could be demanding, anxious, and petulant, more like a needy child than an equal partner. When his girlfriend had had enough of that, she set a boundary and walked away from him. Although she did not do this cleanly, he realized why she had to make the break.

It was a painful but powerful realization for him. He stopped being so angry. Shortly after that, they bumped into each other, and Trevor was able to apologize for his part in their relationship breakdown and own his side of things. They had a painful but honest conversation and parted with more clarity and open-heartedness between them. Trevor was not surprised to see that the cord had changed from heavy, dark, and painful to small and light-filled.

The cord with his mother took a lot longer to heal. Trevor also worked with a therapist and a body worker to heal this childhood trauma. The cord between Trevor and his mother changed as he did the deep work he needed to do to heal from his childhood trauma. He stopped blaming her, and, although not condoning her actions, he was able to feel compassion for her, himself as a child, and their whole family. The cord looked lighter and brighter every time he reached a breakthrough.

Energy cords can linger until we do the work of grieving a lost relationship. Here are some powerful ways to do that.

## Letting Go and Grieving Relationships

One of the biggest struggles that sensitive people face is in letting go of old relationships. As an energy healer, I get constant requests from people who know they need to let go of a past lover, and I feel so much compassion for them, since it's one of the most difficult things to do.

It's not just romantic relationships that are hard to let go of, either. We need to grieve the loss of anyone who was close to us. Family, friends, and even pets can leave a hole in our hearts when they leave that needs attending to.

Sometimes the losses come when someone passes on. People move on in other ways, too; we divorce, drift apart, or become estranged from those we love. We need to heal and let go of those losses or they can continue to drain our energy. And we need a way to do this when we can't actually process the loss with the other person.

One obstacle to clearing old relationships is that we so often didn't get to say what we needed to say to the person. It isn't always realistic or productive to process your feelings with that person, but we do need some way to say it. There is an exercise, called the Seven Day Letter Writing Cure, that I use with my clients and works wonders. It's a miracle for healing grief and also helping us come into a state of forgiveness when harm has been done to us.

# THE SEVEN DAY LETTER WRITING CURE

When we need to let go of someone, clear grief over a lost relationship, or forgive someone who has harmed us—when anger and hurt get jammed up inside us, without a way to express it—we can't heal from relationship loss. This exercise provides a way to fully express our anger, grief, love, and gratitude, and to finally, at the end of the seven days, connect deeply at the soul level. Choose just one person to work on at a time, and if you can, commit to the full seven days.

1.  Begin writing letters to the person: one a day for the first six days. You are *not* going to send the letters, ever, so feel free to let everything out. Don't censor yourself; the goal is to get everything you haven't said off your chest. Lean into it and even exaggerate.

2.  If it's anger you need to express, the first few days' letters will probably be angry ones. Let it rip. Don't show these to anyone else.

3.  Once the anger clears out, you will probably feel hurt. Let out all the hurt into the letters. Be honest. No one will ever read them.

4.  After you have fully expressed the hurt, try reminiscing about the good times and write about any gratitude you have for the person and your relationship. If even the slightest good came out of it, express the gratitude, even if what you learned was how to set a boundary or to be sure of who you *don't* want to be with.

5.  On the seventh day, make your letter a soul-to-soul conversation with this person. If you could bring their soul into your presence, what would you really want to say? Say it as deeply and in as many ways as you can.

6. And then have a funeral for the relationship. Put the letters in a box with any photos you have of the person or objects from them that symbolize the relationship for you, and release the letters in a way that feels safe and final to you: perhaps bury the box in your back yard or burn it on a bonfire.

7. Now celebrate your new life in whatever way you would like: throw a party, have a few friends over. Just remember, under no circumstances share the letters with anyone (except maybe your healer or therapist)—especially not the person you are writing to.

If you carry it all the way through, this can be a very powerful and effective exercise. Chances are good that when you are done, you will have cleared any cords with the person. If you feel like you need to do it again, first give yourself a month off. Try it again until you feel completely clear.

This exercise allows you to fully express all your feelings in a way that provides closure, even in circumstances where you can't do so by talking to the other person. You can do it with people who have died; it's never too late!

Missy is a sensitive and highly creative empath who was left at the altar by her fiancé. Since Missy was nineteen years old and pregnant at the time, this runaway groom left her in a very difficult position. On top of that, Missy's parents refused to help her and her baby. She moved across the country to live with her sister and did her best to put her life back together.

Missy's goal was to open her own spa and hair salon, so she got a job as a hairdresser and went to night school to earn her bachelor's degree in business. As things improved for her and her baby daughter, Missy felt like she was lacking only one thing; a new relationship. She had been so hurt and humiliated by the last one, she felt blocked in this area of her life. Since she wasn't able to contact her former partner, there was no way to process that abrupt ending and get closure.

I asked her if she felt like she needed to evolve the cord between them to its highest level or really release it. Because she had no contact with her ex, she felt she needed to fully release the cord. She did the Seven Day Letter Writing Cure and was able to let go of most of her anger and hurt. After addressing and clearing the lingering pain, Missy was able to express feelings of love and forgiveness to her ex and to thank him and feel grateful for his part in the conception of her beloved daughter. She wished him well on his journey and also set a boundary with him. Since he had walked away, he was not allowed back into their lives in a random or casual way. If he wanted to have a relationship with his daughter, he would need to respect Missy's rules and boundaries around that. As she got clear with her boundaries, she said even more of what she needed to say.

A few days after completing the cure, she received legal documents from her ex, relinquishing his parental rights to their daughter. Although this was painfully final, it was also the outcome that she was hoping for. Not long after this, Missy met a man who became her new partner.

It's very powerful and essential to clear and release old relationships. When we do this, energy cords clear up on their own, and it also can create a space in our hearts and our lives for something new to come in, as was the case for Missy.

Let's end this chapter by taking a look at what can happen when we use love relationships for our highest and best personal and spiritual growth.

## Sacred Sexuality

We have talked about some intense challenges in this chapter. Empaths have the biggest lessons in their primary relationships. We do have a tendency to lose ourselves in these, yet they offer us so much growth as well. Some of our soulmate relationships are harmonious and full of love and support. Other soulmates come to help teach us boundaries. These, the ones that Buddhists call *noble friends*, are there to help us learn better boundaries by challenging our boundaries. This can feel like we are going into the boxing ring for a sparring match.

Like the bully on the playground who knocks you down and steals your lunch money until you take a stand for yourself, these soulmate helpers offer us the friction that we need to find out backbone and our boundary.

The outer world is only a reflection of our inner world. How you love yourself creates a vibration that goes out into the world and draws others to you who will love you the same way that you love yourself. If you don't like yourself very much and don't treat yourself very well, you may attract someone who treats you the same way you are treating yourself.

Our instinct is to try and change the outer world to bring about our happiness. Empaths are easily convinced that we ourselves are the problem; that if we are kind, loving, and caring enough, we can fix or heal someone to the point where they can really love us. We are sure that if we are a better person and we love that energy vampire enough, we will change, save, fix, and heal them with the mighty power of our love.

There are times when that does happen, but both parties must be fully committed to doing the inner work. Let's go instead with the theory that our relationships are a mirror to our inner selves and that which lies hidden and unhealed in us sparks a reaction attraction from your partner. Every point of friction is an opportunity—not to change them, but to look inward and see what is happening inside us that is ready to be healed and released.

# RULES OF CONSCIOUS RELATIONSHIP

⊛ In a conscious relationship, we use the connection that we have with our beloved to work through our own inner process without blaming or projecting on them.

⊛ Many couples realize at some point that they've chosen partners who reflect both good and bad aspects of their respective parents. Their relationship with each other and with us forms much of the background for how we relate to others.

⊛ When there are triggers, we own them as ours and work through them on our own. Once the emotional charge has dissipated, we might choose to share our experience with our partner as an act of intimacy.

⊛ Spiritual partners don't own each other. Ideally, you are cheering your partner on to be their best self and they do the same for you. This requires a deep level of individuation that is difficult for empaths.

⊛ We strive to be deeply honest with each other and have integrity in the relationship. This means establishing guidelines (time, place, consideration for state of mind) for communicating difficult things.

⊛ Real intimacy means having a safe space to reveal all of yourself: emotionally, spiritually, mentally, and physically. This requires work and dedication to the process. Regular time together is key.

⊛ Lies, omissions, and withheld truths create barriers in the relationship that show up in your sex life. Get everything out that needs to be said before sex, and make sure you are kind to each other about it.

As beneficial as all these guidelines are, following them is not always easy, especially if you have years of disconnection between you. If necessary, seek out a good couples' counselor to help you work things through.

In a conscious, spiritual relationship, the partners don't continually blame, complain, and feel victimized, throwing all the responsibility onto their partner and making it a full-time project to force them to change. A real spiritual partnership means that you own all your projections, all your pain, anxiety, and triggers, and that you use the friction in the relationship to work through what is happening inside you.

"You made me feel this way!" gets replaced with "I am having a deep reaction to this and I know it's me and not you. Can we talk about it?" That is where things get really good and start to heal inside both partners.

In this day and age, an alliance of spiritual partners and soulmates seems to last as long as both people continue to grow inside the relationship. When one person stops growing, the relationship may end so that the other can follow their path of growth.

And of course, some people are lucky in love and have wonderful, happy connections with their beloved for their whole lifetime. I believe there is a lot of fate in this aspect of our lives, and it is ruled by our soul contracts with others.

Relationships truly are people growing machines—there are certain spiritual lessons that we can learn only from a deep and heartful connection with another person.

We have covered a lot of information here about how to hold your own in your most intimate relationships. In the next chapter, we will look into what happens when we are so drained that we are in danger of becoming an energy vampire ourself.

# CHAPTER 7

# When Drained, We Drain Others—But We Can Recover

Once, when I taught a workshop on the topic of energy vampires, it was the most sensitive empath in the room who was the biggest energy vampire. Stella was a young woman fresh out of college, and she was very angry at the all horrible vampires in her life. She hadn't yet learned that she could be fully in charge of her own energy and that only she could manage her own boundaries. She was very eager to blame the energy vampires of the world for stealing her energy, all the while clinging to her "poor me" status as an empath. I could see the other workshop participants avoiding her.

As empaths, we may feel that our extreme sensitivity gives us the right to be special and pull energy out of the room, as if sensitivity is a handicap that we are helpless to do anything about. A fully drained empath is like an empty battery that sucks the energy out of an entire room, usually without their even knowing that they are doing it.

## When Empath Becomes Energy Vampire

This can be difficult for empaths to hear, but it's so important to discuss. When an empath has been fully drained by a vampire, or by life itself, they can become an unwitting energy vampire.

Let's look again at the legends of how (supernatural, immortal, bloodsucking) vampires turn their victims into vampires. The seductive, dominating vampire finds a usually willing subject to seduce. It seems clear that blood-sucking vampires would be drawn to the softhearted, easily manipulated empaths. The vampire pours on the sex appeal and charm to mesmerize the empath into willing submission. The vampire then drains their victim to the point of death, until the empath victim actually becomes a vampire too, and that is how vampires are made.

This is also true in the dance of the energy vampire and the empath. If you let yourself be fully drained by an energy vampire, you are in serious danger of becoming one yourself.

And it's not always a vampire who is to blame for draining an empath; you can also be drained by the habit of giving too much or the challenges of a crisis, as well as by life itself in a tough world when you don't know how to manage your energy. Any one of those things can turn an unwary empath into an energy vampire.

It's difficult for empaths to accept that they need to fill their own tank in order to keep going. It seems so selfish to devote time, money, and attention to ourself when so many people in the world need our help. Since empaths feel a spiritual calling to help others, we can easily load up our schedule with too much of a good thing. We give our all at work and then come home and give everything we have left to our families. If we are not careful, all our energy goes out and not enough comes back in, and this creates a critical deficiency in our energy reserves. Our desperate need to restore those depleted reserves can lead us unwittingly into becoming an energy vampire ourself. Here is what to look out for:

- If you are in a long-term relationship with an energy vampire, you are in danger of becoming depleted yourself.

- A strong desire to serve others means we have trouble saying no and can fall prey to habitual over-giving, which can leave us drained.

- Sensitives often feel overwhelmed by their own emotions. Inability to regulate our emotions is also a major energy drain. (See chapter 2 to learn how to manage emotions in a healthier way.)

- On top of all of this, empaths often feel victimized by their own sensitivity and can feel highly disempowered in life. It's tough to love your gift if you have trouble leaving your house, which is true for many sensitives.

Combine all these difficulties, and you have an empath so drained that they are now in serious danger of becoming an energy vampire themself.

So what do we do when we become the victim energy vampire?

## When We Are the Needy, Victim Energy Vampire

It's all too easy to feel victimized by our sensitivity. I am sure that we have all felt that way at some point and wondered why we were being punished. Being an empath can feel like a curse, especially when we don't know how to manage our energy.

In her book *I Don't Want to Be an Empath Anymore: How to Reclaim Your Power Over Emotional Overload, Maintain Boundaries, and Live Your Best Life*,[11] Ora North writes about reclaiming the word *victim*. She says that we have all been victimized by something and we should not try to hide this or sweep it under the rug. There is a shame associated with having a "victim mentality," especially in personal growth and new age circles. Yet chances are very good that you have had some bad stuff happen to you in your life, through no fault of your own. We need to deal with what has happened to us with compassion and with our eyes wide open. We don't pull the punch, makes excuses, and do the spiritual bypass. By fully acknowledging what has happened to us and all the ways that has impacted us, we can move through the experience and fully process it. It needs digesting, and we can do that only by thoroughly examining it with the help of our team of healers.

Here are a few ways to do that.

# EMPOWERMENT PROCESS

Use this any time you notice yourself feeling victimized by something or someone in your life.

1. Take a good look at the situation or person you feel has wounded you and see how this has led you on a path to growth. If you take a big enough step back and look at things from the level of your soul, you might have chosen to experience what you did for a variety of reasons.

2. Let yourself have all your feelings about the situation. Going all the way into pain, grief, and anger can be very empowering. Find safe ways to express your feelings, and get help if you need it. (See chapter 2.)

3. Ask yourself, *What did I learn? How did I grow? Is this an opportunity to heal something or get stronger in some way?*

4. See if you can change your perspective to: *Is there some way that I got myself into this?* and if so, *how I can get myself out?* Of course, any one of us, even the strongest and most aware, can fall on hard times. But taking full responsibility for our actions and choices is how we can leave the victim status behind, *even if all we can change is how we respond to something.*

5. We can feel very empowered by remembering that we have choices. Even if you didn't choose your experience, you can still choose how to respond to it.

6. Get help by finding a therapist, healer, or support group for whatever your original trauma is. Moving on without identifying and acknowledging the original wound is like closing up an abscess that hasn't healed properly.

7. Find a way to help to other people. For most of us, our deepest growth lies in finding a way to help others. Working with those less fortunate than ourself can create a big shift in our perspective.

This empowerment process is very liberating. It can help us release any attachment that we have to our own victim status. But we can't force anyone else to do this deep work; it's up to each of us to do our own work—a difficult truth for us empaths to remember.

I watched in awe as Stella did this. In our workshop, she fully shared with the group all that she had been through. It was the first time Stella told the whole story of her nightmare trauma history to a group of people who actually listened to her. Stella cried about it and expressed her anger too. She was literally and energetically held by the group as she did so. It was so lovely to see her find some inner peace and relief for the pain that she had been carrying all her life.

As she worked through the empowerment process, she saw an opportunity to help other people work through what she had been through. She decided that she would volunteer at her university's crisis center to help others. As Stella fully embraced her past and all its lessons, she finally felt empowered, knowing that what she had been through was part of what made her strong. Her trauma had created a survivor and inspired her to take a powerful direction in her life. With the realization that she was infinitely strong, Stella discovered the key to her life purpose and found a path forward and became not only a survivor but also a *thriver*.

It was amazing to witness her going from being the suckiest victim energy vampire in the room to a strong spiritual warrior.

## Situations Can Turn Us into Vampires, Too

Of course, empaths are not immune to the challenges of life. When those challenges pile up faster than we can process them, we may be in danger of becoming a situational energy vampire. This often follows close on the heels of any kind of change or transition in life, even a good one. Struggling with these changes is not something to feel guilty or wrong about, but we need to notice when it might be happening so we can take steps to help ourself.

When I was going through a painful breakup, I was in danger of becoming a situational energy vampire myself. I really needed to talk to someone every day, but I soon learned that talking to the same person every day put too much of a burden on their time and energy. I rotated around my friends, calling each only about once a week. That meant each had to hear about my struggles only once a week, and in every call, I made sure to also check in with them too on how *their* life was going. I also set myself up with a good therapist and some energy work and buckled down to my self-care.

In a crisis, we tend to drop the very things we need the most, so I made sure I was eating three healthy meals a day, getting plenty of sleep, and still going to the gym. And I doubled down on my meditation and journaling practices. Still, it felt like I was drowning, and the impulse to latch onto another person was strong. But I got through it by using what little strength and discipline I had left to stick to my self-care routine, and that made all the difference.

I believe deeply that we empaths can step up our game and learn to live from a place of empowerment where we fully own our gifts, manage our energy masterfully, and embody all that is wonderful about being an empath. I think of this as living the gift.

We have talked so much about the perils and difficulties of being an empath. Let's spend some time looking at what is fantastic about it!

# Living the Gift

I have a vision of you having accepted all the gifts of being an empath, living fully in your power. In this vision, you are a boundary-setting ninja; with your beautifully strong and flexible energy bubble, you are fully engaged in the world in any way that you want to be. You are not letting your fear make decisions about what you do, where you go, and who you spend time with. When we are spongy, we make those decisions from fear and contraction, but now that you are fully empowered you are living the life you always dreamed that you could.

You have figured out exactly what your brand of empathy is for, and you are saving the planet and its people in your unique way. Because your boundaries and your self-care are excellent, you are filled with soulful joy in your giving. You have learned to give from your full energy tank, stopping when you need to and reveling in the joy and pleasure of recharging.

And you are managing your emotions like a boss, riding their waves and taking all of the pleasure that you can from the sweetness of your own emotional life.

You have chosen relationships that have a life-giving energy balance with people who love you, and you have created healthy boundaries in your more challenging relationships so that people no longer dominate you. You can spot an energy vampire a mile off and avoid them with ease and grace. Since you are the master of your boundaries, there is nothing to fear from people anymore. In fact, you have fallen back in love with the human race, which as an empath is your natural state of being.

On top of all that, you have discovered a tribe of like-minded people who embrace you in meaningful community, and you regularly practice a spiritual discipline that helps keep your spiritual self filled up to the brim with good spiritual juju.

The cherry on top of the sundae is your connection with nature, which also sustains you. You walk in the oxygen-rich woods, through the cool air of the mountains, or along the sunny seashore. Maybe you take your surfboard out every day, trail run, or mountain bike. Perhaps you pull weeds in your vegetable garden, walk your dog, or just hang out on your deck. Nature is a balm to your soul.

You are living the gift. Your empathic nature is your superpower.

We can hold this vision as something to aspire to. Now let's look at a few of the pieces that we haven't covered yet and see how we can get there.

## Living Our Life Purpose

In all my years of working as a psychic, the one question that I get the most from my clients is *What is my life purpose—what am I here for?* It drives people crazy to feel that they are here for a specific purpose but are unable to figure out what that purpose it. We have talked a lot already about how empaths are meant to be healers, helpers, and caretakers, but I believe it is up to us to figure out exactly what our gifts are meant for.

There is no "one size fits all" answer to this question, since everyone has a unique mission, but here are a few thoughts. Our life purpose flows through us in some very powerful and even predictable ways, and there are actually a few different types of empath.

### Nurturing Empaths

Are you a people person? Some empaths have a lot of caretaking energy; they are nurturers. Nurturing empaths have big warm hearts, love to hug people, and often carry motherly or fatherly energy. I fall into this category, since I genuinely love to be around people. If you are a nurturer, you will thrive if you find a way to work directly with people.

Maybe it's in a service industry, as a teacher, or a therapist, or perhaps in the medical field or customer service. If you are in this category, you may really like to work on a team of people, and you will go to great lengths to make sure all your people feel loved and cared about.

## Creative Empaths

Creative empaths love the world of artistic expression: visual, musical, literary. These empaths are so sensitive that working with other adults is sometimes just too much. If you are one of them, you might be called to work with animals, small children, and the elderly. I also see these highly sensitive empaths working as artists, gardeners, musicians, and other highly creative pursuits. Creative empaths may avoid people more than most other empaths and find their true solace in nature and in creativity.

## Warrior Empaths

This may seem like a strange combination, but there are many people who fit into this category; in fact, it might be the most plentiful kind of empath. Warrior empaths are more resilient and naturally stronger than the other types; they choose to use their empathic natures to advocate on behalf of other people. They feel just as deeply and are just as sensitive, but they know that their purpose is to be a spiritual warrior. They thrive in jobs like social work, advocacy, teaching, or speaking to large groups of people. They make great team leaders and use their empathic natures to lead their groups with compassion, making sure everyone's needs are met. They make fierce parents who are protective of their children and also really feel what their children need.

If you want to know more about how to find your life purpose based on what type of person you are, I highly recommend a book by my friend and colleague Rhys Thomas. Rhys created a system of understanding soul types that we use at the Rhys Thomas Institute, the energy medicine school where I teach. Check out his brilliant book *Discover Your Purpose*[12] to find out more about what type of person you might be and how that informs your life purpose.

No matter what kind of empath you are, it's important to remember that your life purpose isn't a *job*; rather, it's a quality of your core self that you can bring to whatever you are doing. If you are a nurturer, you will do that no matter your profession. You may be able to do that better in some jobs than others, but I notice that when people truly accept their core nature, they are automatically drawn to jobs and circumstances that are more resonant and in alignment with that nature.

You don't need a "spiritual" job to live your life purpose. It's better to bring your true spirit into whatever you are doing and try blooming where you are already planted. So many people who have a spiritual awakening feel like they have to quit their day job and become a yoga teacher or a healer or open a healing center. That is fine if that is truly what you feel called to do, but I love to see people bring their natural empathic healing skills to wherever they already are. Many empaths are meant to bring their healing mojo to their families, to their corporate job, or to their friends and neighborhood communities. It's a kind of street ministry—bringing the healing to people where they are. Empaths are spread out all over the world, bringing their love and healing energy to wherever they are, and that is a beautiful thing. You may be planted where you are to bring your healing ability right there, right where it is needed most.

I see many very powerful healers in corporate jobs right now. I think there is a purpose to this. Corporations are so powerful now, and many of them are waking up and choosing to create more conscious connections to their employees, their customers, and the planet. Maybe you are there with a wave of other empaths, helping those big, powerful entities make better decisions and come further into the light. It's so hopeful that many of them want to. They are choosing inclusivity policies, encouraging women's leadership, and greening their practices. If that is where you are, it may be that you are meant to help steer corporate culture onto a gentler and more thoughtful path. Think of the powerful collective impact that can have.

Don't automatically quit your corporate job; if you bring your real self and practice all the energy management skills we have learned, the corporate realm might be the perfect place for you to share your gifts. And if it isn't, then staying in your core self and your heart will help lead you to a job that is more resonant for you. Again, your life purpose isn't really a job; it's you being deeply, passionately, and unapologetically yourself, no matter where you are and what you are doing.

I have a lovely office and see clients all week, yet I know that you could take me out of my office and put me anywhere else and I would still be giving people Reiki and talking to their dearly departed. It's not so much what I do as who I am. My life purpose is to help people like you, training emerging empaths, healers, and psychics to fully step into their gifts, because the world needs all the healers it can get, and you are my people. That is what is in my core, and I will bring it anywhere I go.

Consider what this might be for you. Chances are very good that you have been doing it all along anyway.

I hope that this conversation will help you figure out your life purpose. It is one of the most powerful things you can do find happiness in your life.

Now let's talk about another key need that many empaths miss in their lives.

## Meaningful Community

Far too many of us have been isolated in unhealthy ways. While it's true that many empaths are introverted, that doesn't mean that we don't need and deserve to be a part of a meaningful community. Empaths love deep emotional connection with others, and for this we often prefer a one-on-one connection—perhaps because we hate small talk and shallow connection. Perhaps we avoid casual social connections because they are too surface for our deep natures.

My friend and fellow healer Eric dislikes social interactions like that. "I hate parties, mostly because I don't want to talk about football scores or what kind of car someone is driving. I hate arguing about politics, or arguing about anything, really. I want to talk about deep and meaningful topics, which is not accepted in casual social interactions, especially with other men."

But Eric did find what he was looking for when he joined a few Meetup groups. Eric is a creative and nature-loving empath, so he found one nearby group called "Nature Loving Empaths Who Hike" and another one about energy medicine. These groups put him in touch with like-minded folks who shared the same values and experiences.

Empaths often feel that they need to pretend to be something they are not and that they are alone in the world. We can feel like misfits and even social outcasts. The good news is that these days we can find communities all over. They might be meditation groups, Reiki shares, or church groups. Look into yoga classes, or find the spiritual hub in your town and check out their bulletin boards. And check online for Meetups or Facebook groups where you can get support and find a community.

It's incredibly healing for empaths to come out of the spiritual closet and find a group of others who can validate their experiences and understand where they are coming from. Search for some meaningful community. We all need it.

Next up, let's look into the importance of a deep and abiding spiritual practice.

## Spiritual Practice

For empaths to thrive, we must have a way to reconnect our energy to something greater than ourselves. While all people need this, empaths have a deep core need to reconnect to their source energy; it's a necessary and healthy way to refill our energy tanks. People become energy vampires in part because they don't know how to refill their own energy from the two major sources that are available to all of us. These sources are spiritual energy and the energy of the natural world, earth energy. If we forget how to replenish ourselves from these sources, we may develop a bad habit of stealing energy from other people.

If we are to live fully empowered lives, we must reconnect on a regular basis to these unlimited supplies of energy. Spiritual practice can be anything that helps reconnect you on a regular basis to your fundamental source of spirit energy. It can be a more traditional religious worship at a church, temple, or mosque. Perhaps you are more drawn to Eastern practices like yoga, tai chi, or qigong. Whatever you are drawn to, make it a regular practice.

Meditation practices are so healing and powerful that I recommend them to everyone. There are many ways to do meditation, from an easy app on your phone to meditation groups and classes, all the way to formal practices that take lifetimes to master. I think that we each need to learn a method that works for us, and it's very beneficial to study with a teacher in a system with some structure, at least while we are learning.

If you have an extra-busy mind, try a mantra-based practice, or pray the rosary or do some chanting. Sound practices tend to slow down the mind and give us something besides our thoughts to focus on.

For those of us who are very ungrounded and out of body habitually, a body-based practice like yoga is better. This will help reconnect your mind with your whole body and create integration throughout your being.

# THE BENEFITS OF MEDITATION

Meditation is an essential way for empaths to reconnect to our spiritual power source. It takes discipline to stick to a daily practice, but the rewards are powerfully healing:

- Meditation helps empaths learn to experience our thoughts and feelings but not overly identify with them; to see that we have them, but they are not the whole of us. This allows us to be a compassionate witness to our self and gives us access to our own inner wisdom as we begin to recognize our old unconscious patterns and responses. We can then choose to let those go and live more in the present moment.

- Meditation allows us the quiet and receptive time that we need to tune in to our inner guidance system so that we can connect with our guidance and our own intuition. Meditation is one of the best tools to increase your psychic and intuitive ability.

- It has been proven, over and over, that meditation is highly beneficial for our physical health, lowering blood pressure and stress hormones. As we relax more, our body activates its own natural healing mechanisms, including the immune system.

- Big improvements in our mental health are also possible; many studies show a significant decrease in anxiety and depression for those who follow a meditation practice.

- There is evidence that regular meditation helps with recovery from addiction, increases your attention span, and slows age-related memory loss.

Whichever way you find suits you best, meditation is good for all of you!

I have been trained in many meditation techniques through the years, and I mostly work with a breath-based meditation, breathing up my spine in the inhale and focusing my attention on the exhale breath. I meditate for at least twenty minutes a day, sometimes more. I prefer to meditate right before bedtime; I feel this clears out my energy field, emotions, and thoughts, and that allows me to sleep better. I always start this with the grounding and clearing practice that we learned in chapter 3.

I try to meditate in the same place in my house. I use a cushion to sit on; if that is difficult for you, a chair is just as good. I keep my journal close by, and if I feel emotionally cluttered and overwhelmed, I will pour out my emotions into my journal until I feel clear and then go back to meditating. It has taken me many years to find a practice that works for me, and I change it up when I need to. I urge you to try out different practices until you find something that works for you, then stick with it.

Meditation is one way to connect to a never-ending and universal power source. The other way—connecting with nature—belongs on every empath's "must have" list.

## Connecting with Nature

There is no doubt about it: finding some time to connect to the natural world is balm for the soul of most empaths. Being in nature helps us ground, breathe, and release all the accumulated energy that we have picked up from other sources.

For me, it's being out in the woods or at the beach. There is conservation land just down the street from my house, a beautiful New England forest around a lake, and I need to go in there as often as I can. About fifteen minutes into my walk, I can feel my energy field release all the emotional goo that I have been holding on to from other people and the places I have been. I can feel myself drop into my body again, and I can let my energy field expand out to its natural diffuse, spread-out form.

The woods are full of oxygen, ozone, and negative ions, which are calming and soothing to our sensitive energy fields. The Japanese call it forest bathing, and they prescribe for all kind of physical and mental health issues. I know that I go into the woods feeling all tangled up and come out feeling like myself again, even after only thirty minutes of walking there. I have good rain and snow gear, and you will find me there pretty much every day, all year round, even here in New England where we have long, frigid winters.

Being in nature should be on the prescription list for any empath who can swing it. In an ideal world, we would all be able to find a way to do that; even empaths who live in urban environments can still find a way to get into nature. Parks abound in most cities, with more rural places nearby.

Some empaths thrive in their own backyard gardens and green-houses, but even if you can't get out much, you can still enjoy window boxes and houseplants. Bring nature indoors and see if you feel better.

In addition to plants and the outdoors, empaths have a special bond with animals, and many enjoy their pets as much as they enjoy other humans, if not more so. Domesticated animals like horses, dogs, and cats go particularly well with empaths, who can use their gifts to connect with their pets. Empaths are the natural-born animal whisper-ers of the world; our ability to feel what they feel and catch their thoughts is built into our empathic gifts.

Wherever you live or whatever kind of nature is around you, getting yourself out there is a primal way to restore your energy reserves. We need a steady flow of both the ineffable and the earthly energies flowing through us.

We are all wired to have otherworldly energy flowing in the top of the head, winding through the chakras, and leaving the body through the soles of the feet. This is part of the reason it's so important to take off your shoes and put your bare feet on the ground as often as you can. Earthly energy comes up from the feet, winds its way through the chakras, and emerges out the top of the head. So we are truly like a lightning rod, mixing those energies through and being fed by them. As we reignite that pattern, we can keep our energy clear and full.

I hope this chapter has given you some vital information that you can use to avoid becoming an energy vampire yourself, and that you can now live your life as an empath honoring your sensitivity as your superpower, because it truly is just that.

We started out talking about Lily as an example of an empath feeling swamped by her sensitivity. I promised we would find out what happened to her as she did this work. This will be my closing gift for you.

# Conclusion

Remember Lily from chapter 1? Let's explore how she used the material that we covered in the book to help her live an empowered life as an empath.

Lily took to heart the energy management exercises that we learned in chapter 3 and began to practice them daily. Almost immediately, she began to have better boundaries. She learned how to say no to the difficult people in her life, and she was shocked to find that, after their initial outburst about the change, they actually started to respect her.

"My boss and my mother have both learned how much I am willing to give and where my edge is now. When they try to push me around, I stick to my guns and have learned a few kind, but very firm ways to say no. It's amazing that we all get along better now, and I don't absolutely dread going in to work anymore."

Lily used the bubble and energy clearing exercises to release all the negative energy she picked up by being in the world. "I would sit in my car after work and release any leftover work energy down into the earth before I drove home. And I cut cords every day too." This practice helped Lily let go of her work day, and she stopped bringing her work home with her, both emotionally and energetically. "That played a big part in keeping the boundary of work away from my home life. I stopped resenting work and remembered that I actually love my job because I truly like helping people. What a relief!"

Lily said that she also started to feel stronger and more resilient emotionally. The work that we did in chapter 2 gave her a daily practice to process her emotions—to digest them as she needed to. "This became part of a daily ritual. I would journal every day about how I felt and really let it all out, without judgment. That is when I noticed how rich my emotional life really is and how connected to my intuition it is."

A few months into this practice, Lily told me that her anxiety levels had dropped so much that, with the help of her doctor, she was tapering off her anti-anxiety medications. As Lily also learned how to replace her lost energy, much of her fatigue disappeared. She spent her free time playing with her son, mostly outside in nature, and that helped keep her energy tanks full.

"I started napping when Adam napped and playing with him when he played, and we both felt so much better," Lily said. "I learned to accept that I need that rest and play and to allow myself to have it instead of pushing all the time."

The final piece of the puzzle for her was sticking to a cleaner diet and cutting out as many chemicals as possible out of her life. Since empaths are very sensitive to chemicals, food additives, and electromagnetic radiation like WiFi, Lily also noticed a significant improvement when she consumed more organic foods, cut down on her chemical load, and turned off her WiFi at night.

Lily summed up her experience this way: "I was sure that I was emotionally broken and sort of crazy. I felt so abnormally sensitive and could never figure out why I wasn't like other people. I wasn't able to be strong and handle life in a normal way like everyone else did. Other people didn't have a mini nervous breakdown by just going to the supermarket and running errands, but those things would leave me flat out for the rest of the day. Now that I have had the energy management training, I appreciate my sensitive nature. It makes me a great mother, and I am really good at my job, which is all about helping people. I needed to learn to accept that about myself and to care for myself every day, and now I love being an empath!"

It was inspiring and gratifying to watch Lily fully empower herself and embrace her empathic nature. My deepest wish for you is that you find the same loving acceptance of yourself as an empath. The world needs you to go out and find the people and situations that you are meant to help. As you stand in your sensitivity—your superpower—I know that you will be out there with all the other empaths, saving the world.

# Acknowledgments

I feel so much gratitude for anyone who reads my books. Writers need readers, just as teachers need students. Thank you for helping me complete my life purpose by doing so.

Big squishy love and gratitude to my book-writing fairy godparents, Kelly Sullivan Walden and Jacob Nordby. Thank you both so much for inspiring me to keep writing and for holding my hand through gritty bits. Kelly, heartfelt thanks for the beautiful foreword.

Special thanks to Ogmios for getting the illustrations exactly right. Thank you, Kelley Twombly, for always having my back. And many thanks to my family, Bill and Jennifer Campion and my sister, Sara Campion-Egan, for the unconditional support. All my love to my children, Grayson, Devin, and Genevieve, who taught me so much about both love and boundary setting.

And to my friends, for your patience when I need to put everything down and just write.

To my New Harbinger family: you are the best!

# Endnotes

1 Elaine N. Aron, PhD, *The Highly Sensitive Person: How to Thrive When the World Overwhelms You* (New York: Broadway Books, 1997).

2 Judith Orloff, MD, *The Empath's Survival Guide: Life Strategies for Sensitive People* (Louisville, CO: Sounds True, 2018).

3 Masaru Emoto, *The Hidden Messages in Water* (New York: Atria Books, 2005).

4 Eileen Day McKusick, *Tuning the Human Biofield: Healing with Vibrational Sound Therapy* (New York: Healing Arts Press, 2014).

5 Christiane Northrup, MD, *Dodging Energy Vampires: An Empath's Guide to Evading Relationships that Drain You and Restoring Your Health and Power* (Carlsbad, CA: Hay House, 2019).

6 American Psychiatric Association, *Diagnostic and Statistical Manual of Mental Disorders*, 5th ed. (Washington, DC: American Psychiatric Association, 2013).

7 Ross Rosenburg, MEd, *The Human Magnet Syndrome: The Codependent Narcissist Trap* (New York: Morgan James Publishing, 2018).

8 Emma Chan, *Narcissist Abuse Recovery: A Guide to Finding Clarity and Reclaiming Your Joy After Leaving a Toxic Relationship* (self-published, 2018).

9 Caroline Myss, PhD, *Why People Don't Heal and How They Can* (New York: Harmony Publishing, 1998).

10 David Schnarch, *Passionate Marriage: Keeping Love and Intimacy Alive in Committed Relationships*, reprint ed. (New York: Norton, 2009).

11 Ora North, *I Don't Want to Be an Empath Anymore: How to Reclaim Your Power Over Emotional Overload, Maintain Boundaries, and Live Your Best Life* (Oakland, CA: Reveal Press, 2019).

12 Rhys Thomas, *Discover Your Purpose: How to Use the 5 Life Purpose Profiles to Unlock Your Hidden Potential and Live the Life You Were Meant to Live* (New York: TarcherPerigee, 2015).

**Lisa Campion** is a psychic counselor and Reiki master teacher with more than twenty-five years of experience. She has trained more than one thousand practitioners in the hands-on, energy-healing practice of Reiki, including medical professionals; and has conducted more than fifteen thousand individual sessions in her career. Based near Providence, RI, she specializes in training emerging psychics, empaths, and healers so they can fully step into their gifts—the world needs all the healers it can get!

# MORE BOOKS for the SPIRITUAL SEEKER

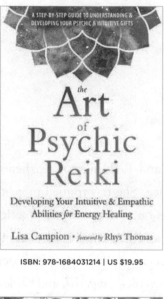

ISBN: 978-1684031214 | US $19.95

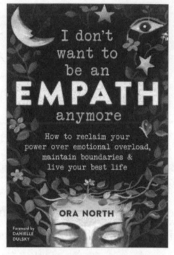

ISBN: 978-1684034178 | US $16.95

ISBN: 978-1684035304 | US $16.95

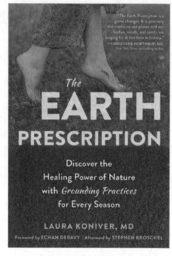

ISBN: 978-1684034895 | US $17.95

## newharbingerpublications

NON-DUALITY PRESS | REVEAL PRESS